Grammar Tales

by Pamela Chanko

New York • Toronto • London • Auckland • Sydney
New Delhi • Mexico City • Hong Kong • Buenos Aires

Teaching *Resources*

Cover and interior design by NEO Grafika .
Illustrations by Doug Jones, Kelly Kennedy, Jared Lee, and Matt Phillips

ISBN 0-439-45827-7
Copyright © 2004 by Scholastic Inc.
All rights reserved.
Printed in China.

1 2 3 4 5 6 7 8 9 10   40   11 10 09 08 07 06 05 04

Table of Contents

A Note to Teachers

The word *grammar* has been known to inspire groans in many a classroom—from students and teachers alike! A "grammar lesson" conjures up images of tedious worksheets and lists of disconnected rules that appear to have no meaning in "real" life—and thus are easily forgotten. Yet it is undeniable that using good grammar—and understanding its rules—is an important real-life skill, and one which every student needs in order to succeed. So how can we help students see the importance of learning grammar? How can we help them connect these skills to their everyday lives?

The key lies in putting grammar in *context*. Learning grammatical rules through isolated exercises can get a bit boring. In addition, its success rate is rather hit or miss. Why? Disconnected information is unlikely to stick with students for long. But when students are able to connect the rules of grammar with real reading and writing, the picture changes. Language begins to come to life as students see for themselves the power of a strong verb in action, or the descriptive ability of a well-chosen adjective. That's where the *Grammar Tales* program comes in. By placing grammatical concepts in the context of engaging stories and hands-on activities, *Grammar Tales*™ helps students see the true power of language—and the power of using it well.

Why is learning grammar important? Many students might argue that technology has superceded the need for learning basic language rules. After all, most computer word-processing programs have built-in tools to correct common errors. However, a computer cannot teach students how to express themselves with fluency and flair. Learning the basic rules of grammar—including parts of speech, punctuation, and sentence structure—enables students to become better writers and better speakers.

When students are armed with good communication skills, they increase their chances of success in every subject area. Although a grasp of content is important, most teachers believe that well-expressed ideas are equally important. Knowing basic English grammar can also help students master foreign languages more easily. And later in life, a well-written letter or an articulate interview can open the door to a new opportunity. There is also an immediate, practical reason to include grammar in the curriculum: school districts across the country are giving students standardized tests in grammar and composition at increasingly early grade levels. Students need direct instruction in order to succeed on these tests.

In addition, grammar instruction gives students and teachers a common language with which to talk about their reading and writing. Once students understand what a verb is, for instance, teachers can help them choose a more descriptive one for a sentence. Once they understand the definition of a run-on sentence, students can learn how to avoid them in their own writing.

Grammar Tales™ takes the mystery and fear out of learning proper language usage by making these abstract concepts accessible and concrete for students. And, perhaps most importantly, it takes the tedium out of this much-dreaded subject by making grammar *fun and funny*. So invite students to get in on the grammar game as they learn to love language with *Grammar Tales*™!

Welcome to Grammar Tales

Most teachers agree that direct instruction in grammar is essential in helping students master proper use of the English language. Learning grammar enables students to become better writers, better speakers, and more successful learners. However, teaching grammar also presents instructors with a major challenge: the announcement of a grammar lesson is often greeted with yawns and even some eye-rolling. There's no doubt about it—grammar is a necessary part of the curriculum. But does it have to be so bland? The answer is no! There is a way to make learning grammar fun. Let Grammar Tales™ come to the rescue!

Grammar Tales™ is a series of stories that teach the basic elements of grammar in a fun and innovative way. Each title focuses on a specific concept, from parts of speech to punctuation. The 10 titles in the series provide engaging instruction on the following topics:

- **Nouns**
- **Verbs**
- **Adjectives**
- **Adverbs**
- **Pronouns**
- **Capitalization**
- **Commas**
- **Quotation Marks**
- **Sentence Structure**
- **Proofreading**

You may already be teaching some or all of these concepts in your classroom. Or you may be searching for a way to make grammar more interesting and accessible to students. What is the *Grammar Tales*™ difference? By embedding grammatical concepts in stories that feature engaging plots, friendly, lovable characters, and lots of good humor, these books make the rules of language come alive in your classroom. They allow—and encourage—students to think about grammar and language in a whole new way.

For instance, what would the world be like if no one used pronouns? Students can visit *The Planet Without Pronouns* to find out! How can something as small as a comma accomplish such great deeds in a sentence? Just read about this tiny hero's adventures in *When Comma Came to Town*. Can a verb really help stave off boredom? In *A Verb for Herb*, students see for themselves how these little words inject plenty of exciting action into one boy's ordinary day. Each story provides a concrete context for what might otherwise be an abstract concept, making the rules of grammar more likely to stick with students. Each story also includes an interactive element: questions and activities in the sidebars invite students to become part of the reading experience and practice using their new knowledge as they read.

In addition to the storybooks, the *Grammar Tales*™ program includes mini-lessons, puzzles, and extension activities to reinforce and enhance students' learning. You'll find everything you need in this teaching guide. The following features are included for each title in the series:

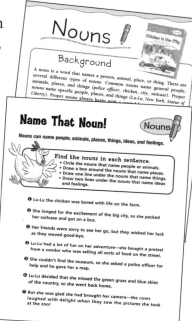

- **Lesson Plans:** This section begins with background information on the topic, including definitions, terminology, and basic rules. Next, you'll find a detailed lesson plan for the book, including Before Reading discussions, During Reading strategies, and After Reading extension activities.

- **Overheads:** This reproducible page provides an opportunity for whole-group instruction. Using an overhead projector, you can work with students to mark up sentences and paragraphs using the knowledge and skills they've learned from the story. These reproducibles can also be used as independent practice sheets.

- **Mini-Books:** Included in this guide is a complete, reproducible mini-version of each title in the series. Students can build their own mini-book collection, and read the books both in school and at home with their families.

- **Mini-Book Activities:** Each mini-book is also an interactive activity book. Following the story, students will find five pages of activities, including puzzles, games, and challenging quizzes to test their new knowledge.

- **Answer Keys:** Answers for the overhead pages and mini-book puzzles are included in the back of this guide.

You will find that the overheads and mini-book activities also feature the characters from the stories, making each unit of study cohesive. For instance, after reading *Francine Fribble, Proofreading Policewoman*, the reproducible gives students the opportunity to proofread a new paragraph about Francine's adventures. You will find that this not only provides continuity, but also helps keep the fun going during your lessons—keeping students engaged and their interest levels high.

On the following pages, teaching tips will help you get the most out of each element of the *Grammar Tales*™ program in your classroom. You will find that the lessons and activities are not only quick and easy, but also a lot of fun to teach. *Grammar Tales*™ can open up a whole new world of language (and laughter!) for you and your students. So the next time you announce a grammar lesson, you just might be greeted with a round of applause instead of yawns!

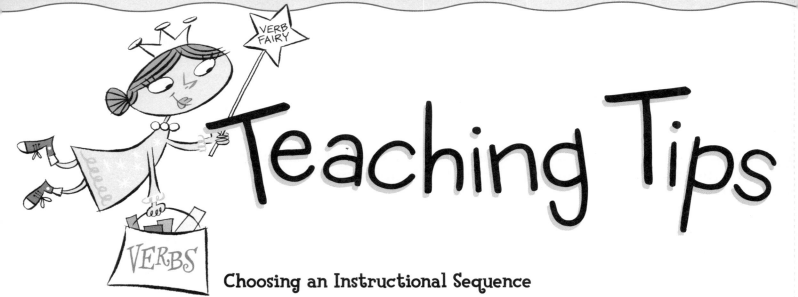

Teaching Tips

Choosing an Instructional Sequence

There is no "correct" order for teaching elements of grammar to students. As a teacher, you are the best judge of what your students need and when they need it. You will find that the lessons in this guide fall into two main categories: parts of speech (the first five lessons) and punctuation and structure (the last five lessons). Some teachers feel it is best to begin with parts of speech, because these concepts are more concrete. Learning to recognize, define, and use parts of speech correctly (such as nouns and verbs) can provide students with a strong framework as they move into more abstract areas such as sentence structure and comma placement.

However, you may find that the most effective method for choosing your instructional sequence is to pay close attention to your students' writing. For instance, if you find that students are having trouble distinguishing proper from common nouns, you might take this as your cue to introduce a lesson on capitalization. If you find structural errors (such as run-on sentences) in students' writing, this may mean that they are experimenting with more complex language—and are therefore ready for a lesson on sentence structure. Remember that errors in students' work are not cause for distress—rather, they are clues to their development as writers. As students' use of language becomes more sophisticated and complex, there are bound to be errors in their punctuation and usage. This simply means that they are ready for additional instruction that they can apply to their own work.

Using the Books

In this guide you will find specific lesson plans for each *Grammar Tales*,™ including Before, During, and After Reading strategies. Following are some general tips to keep in mind as you use the books with students.

Before Reading

• It is always a good idea to find out what students already know about a topic before you begin instruction. You might write the topic on the board (for instance, the word *Adjective*) and invite students to share their ideas. Are they familiar with the term? How would they define it? Use students' responses to guide the pace and content of your lesson.

- Show students the cover of the book before you begin reading. Invite them to make predictions about the story's characters, setting, and plot. You might write students' predictions on a sheet of chart paper. Refer to the list after reading to see how many of their predictions were correct.

- Invite students to make predictions about the story that focus on the grammatical element being taught. For instance, what adverbs might describe how Tillie plays her tuba? What nouns might Lu-Lu see on her trip to the city?

During Reading

- During the first reading, simply read the story text aloud while allowing students to look at the illustrations. Give them time to become engaged in the story and language.

- During subsequent readings, invite students to participate by reading the information in the sidebars. Encourage students to respond to any questions and try out the mini-activities suggested.

- Encourage students to be active readers and listeners by asking their own questions as well. Stop to clarify any points in the story text or sidebars as needed.

After Reading

- Invite students to take on the roles of the characters and act out the story. You can provide additional writing practice by challenging students to create play scripts for their performances.

- Invite students to write and/or perform a continuation of the story. For instance, what town might Comma visit next? What will she do there?

- Help students connect the concepts in the book to their own writing. For instance, after reading *Francine Fribble, Proofreading Policewoman*, students can choose a piece of writing from their portfolio to proofread and correct, using what they've learned from the story. After reading *The Bug Book*, students can underline all the adjectives they used in a piece of independent writing, and perhaps replace them with more descriptive ones. Using what they've learned to improve earlier pieces of writing will help students internalize the concepts and see their practical, real-world applications.

Using the Overheads

Following the lesson plan for each title, you will find a reproducible activity sheet to use with students. This sheet is designed to provide additional hands-on practice in each given topic: students are invited to mark up the page using the concepts they've learned from the story. For instance, the activity sheet for *Chicken in the City* invites students to read a set of sentences and identify the different types of nouns in each. After reading the *No-Good, Rotten, Run-On Sentence*, students have the opportunity to identify and repair run-on sentences. Correct answers to the activity sheets are provided in the back of this guide. There are several ways to use the overhead reproducibles:

•**Group Overhead Activity:** Use the activity sheet with an overhead projector for group instruction. Simply copy the sheet onto transparency film and place it on the bed of your projector. Read the directions aloud with students. Then invite students to take turns coming up to the projector and marking up the page as directed, using a dry-erase marker. (Alternatively, you can have students raise their hands with suggestions and mark up the page yourself.) Encourage students to articulate the reasons behind their suggestions, and discuss them as a class. For instance, why should a particular word in a sentence be capitalized while another should not? How did students decide where a comma should be placed?

•**Guided Practice:** Make one copy of the activity sheet for each student and guide students through the lesson as they mark up their own pages. You can do this in conjunction with an overhead projector or without one.

•**Independent Practice:** Give students a copy of the activity sheet and invite them to complete the activity independently. You might choose to use the sheets as an assessment tool, noting students' responses to gauge their grasp of the material. You might also use students' completed activity sheets as a basis for individual conferences. Discuss students' responses and the reasons behind their choices.

Using the Mini-Books

Included in this guide is a complete reproducible mini-version of each title in the series. The mini-books provide an excellent way to reinforce students' learning, as well as a way to build home-school connections. Following are a few suggestions for using the mini-books in your program.

•After reading a *Grammar Tale* with the group, invite students to create their own copy (see *How to Assemble the Mini-Books* on page 11). Students can then follow along in their mini-books as you read the story again. Invite students to use their mini-books to participate in the reading. For instance, while reading *The Bug Book*, invite students to point to each adjective they see in their own books as you read the text aloud.

•As you teach each concept, build a learning center for additional independent practice. The mini-books can be used as the basis for an activity. Set out copies of the books and invite students to mark up the pages to show what they've learned. For instance, they might circle each noun they see in *Chicken in the City*, or proofread the text in *Francine Fribble, Proofreading Policewoman*.

•Have each student bring in a shoe box from home and use it to build a personal grammar library. If they wish, students can decorate their boxes with art materials. In addition to their copies of the mini-books, students can use the box to store favorite writing samples, or pieces of writing they'd like to revise. They can then use their mini-book library for reference as they edit their work.

• Invite students to take copies of the mini-books home to share with family members. To involve family members further, write instructions for a quick activity they can do with students at home. For instance, you might invite family members to go on a scavenger hunt for nouns in each room of their home. Place the activity and a copy of the mini-book in a zip-close bag to create your own take-home packs.

Using the Mini-Book Activities

Each mini-book in the series is also an interactive activity book. Following each story, you will find five mini-pages of puzzles and games to reinforce and extend students' understanding of the concepts in the story. Each game has easy-to-follow instructions for students printed right on the page to encourage independent learning. Correct answers are provided at the back of this guide. You might choose to provide the puzzle pages as an option for learning-center work, or assign them as homework. Any way you choose to use them, these activities are sure to add fun and interest to your program. You will find the following puzzle formats included in the mini-books:

• **Crosswords:** These puzzles are designed to help students recognize—and use—each part of speech featured in the series: nouns, verbs, adjectives, adverbs, and pronouns. Students are given clues in the form of incomplete sentences. Students choose a word from the box to complete each sentence correctly, and then write the word in the crossword grid. Each clue and answer is related directly to the grammatical concept—there are no "filler" words.

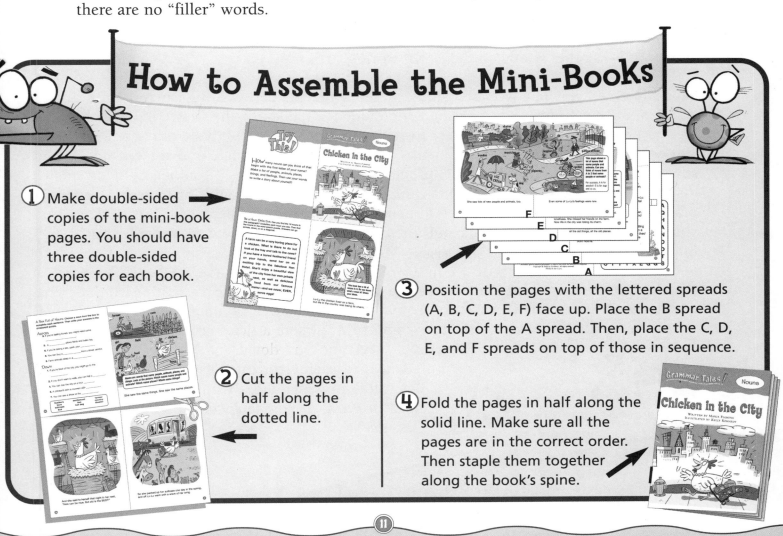

How to Assemble the Mini-Books

① Make double-sided copies of the mini-book pages. You should have three double-sided copies for each book.

② Cut the pages in half along the dotted line.

③ Position the pages with the lettered spreads (A, B, C, D, E, F) face up. Place the B spread on top of the A spread. Then, place the C, D, E, and F spreads on top of those in sequence.

④ Fold the pages in half along the solid line. Make sure all the pages are in the correct order. Then staple them together along the book's spine.

- **Word Searches:** These puzzles are also designed to help students recognize parts of speech. Students are invited to read a humorous paragraph (each is a story-related "advertisement") and underline each word that corresponds with the specified part of speech. Students then hunt for each underlined word in the word search grid. Answers can go across, down, or diagonally.

- **Secret Message Quizzes:** These games are designed to help students recognize proper usage of punctuation and structure. The quizzes are in multiple-choice format; students are asked to fill in the bubble next to the sentence that uses correct grammar. Students then use the letters of their answer choices to decode a congratulatory secret message.

- **Try This!:** On the back cover of each mini-book, students will find a quick idea for a fun, independent extension activity. For instance, students are invited to write an acrostic adjective poem about themselves, create a list of nouns beginning with the first letter of their names, and so on.

Assessment

The overhead reproducible activity sheets and mini-book activity pages included in this guide can help you to assess students' progress. Students' responses on the reproducible activity sheets, as well as their ability to solve the mini-book puzzles, will certainly give you valuable information and help you to plan upcoming lessons. However, the best way to track students' true grasp of grammatical concepts is to look at their independent writing. After all, the real test of students' learning lies in whether or not they can apply it to real-world situations—in other words, to their own work.

Set aside time every few weeks to study students' independent writing carefully. You might create a three-column record sheet: write students' names in the first column, label the second column Strengths, and label the third column Needs. As you read each student's work, keep notes on their key strengths and needs. For instance, one student might use adjectives to great effect, but be prone to run-on sentences. Another student might demonstrate a good grasp of capitalization rules, but have trouble with correct comma placement. You can use your notes to plan individual mini-conferences with students. As you discuss their work, point out their strengths in addition to providing tips for improvement in needed areas.

Another useful assessment tool is to keep a class "error-tally." Collect a writing sample from each student and create a list of common errors, such as mispunctuated dialogue, capitalization mistakes, and so on. Make a tick mark on the list for each error you see, and jot down the appropriate students' initials next to each error category. Tally your results to determine in which areas whole-group instruction is most needed, or organize small groups for mini-lessons.

Nouns

Background

A noun is a word that names a person, animal, place, or thing. There are several different types of nouns. Common nouns name general people, animals, places, and things (*police officer*, *chicken*, *city*, *suitcase*). Proper nouns name specific people, places, and things (*Lu-Lu*, *New York*, *Statue of Liberty*). Proper nouns always begin with a capital letter. Concrete nouns name things you can see, hear, smell, touch, or taste, while abstract nouns name feelings or ideas (*excitement*, *charm*, *life*). Nouns can be singular (*farm*) or plural (*friends*). You and your students will find examples of each type of noun included in the story.

Before Reading

- Introduce the book to students by beginning a discussion about a trip they took recently (such as a class trip or a family vacation). Ask: *Who went on the trip? Where did you go? What things did you see there?* Write students' responses on the board under the headings *People*, *Places*, and *Things*. Then read the lists together and explain that each list contains words that are nouns. A noun is a word that names a *person*, *animal*, *place*, or *thing*.

- You might also choose to point out any proper nouns on the list and help students distinguish them from common nouns. Explain that common nouns are general words (*teacher*, *museum*), while proper nouns are specific names (*Mrs. Smith*, *Natural History Museum*). Point out that proper nouns are always capitalized.

- Next, show students the cover of the book and invite them to make predictions about the story. What people, animals, places, and things do they think Lu-Lu will see on her trip?

During Reading

After reading the story once through for meaning, you can reinforce a variety of concepts in subsequent readings.

- Invite students to raise their hands each time they hear any type of noun.

- Reinforce different types of nouns by having students raise their hands only when they hear a place noun. Then try the same technique for animal nouns, feeling nouns, idea nouns, and so on.

- Point out the difference between singular nouns and plural nouns. Students can clap their hands once for singulars and twice for plurals.

After Reading

In addition to the group overhead lesson and mini-book practice activities, try the following extensions to help reinforce students' learning.

- Play a game of categories. Have students write several noun categories across the top of a sheet of paper (such as *People*, *Animals*, *Foods*, *Places*, and *Feelings*). Then choose three or four random letters of the alphabet to write down the left side of the paper. Set a time limit, such as five or ten minutes, and challenge students to write a noun in the grid for each category beginning with the letter in each row.

- Go on a noun scavenger hunt. Divide the class into small groups and assign each a different area of the classroom. Have each group create a list of all the nouns they found in their area. Compare lists as a class. Which group found the most nouns?

- What people, places, and things might Lu-Lu have seen if she had taken a trip to your neighborhood? Invite students to create noun-filled travel brochures for their community. They can illustrate and label people, places, and things a visitor might see. For an extra challenge, invite students to work abstract nouns into their brochures as well. For instance, a caption might read: *Life in Hartsdale is full of excitement!*

To Extend Learning

Use the activity on the next page to reinforce and extend the concepts students have learned. You can turn this into a collaborative class activity by using the page on an overhead projector, or make multiple copies for students to work on individually.

- Have students read the directions at the top of the sheet. Then have them read each sentence and point out the nouns.

- Invite volunteers to mark up each sentence as directed, indicating the different types of nouns they find: people and animals, places, things, or ideas and feelings. Encourage students to explain their reasoning as they make their markings. How can they tell which category each noun belongs to?

Name That Noun!

Nouns can name people, animals, places, things, ideas, and feelings.

Find the nouns in each sentence.
- Circle the nouns that name people or animals.
- Draw a box around the nouns that name places.
- Draw one line under the nouns that name things.
- Draw two lines under the nouns that name ideas and feelings.

❶ Lu-Lu the chicken was bored with life on the farm.

❷ She longed for the excitement of the big city, so she packed her suitcase and got on a bus.

❸ Her friends were sorry to see her go, but they wished her luck as they waved good-bye.

❹ Lu-Lu had a lot of fun on her adventure—she bought a pretzel from a vendor who was selling all sorts of food on the street.

❺ She couldn't find the museum, so she asked a police officer for help and he gave her a map.

❻ Lu-Lu decided that she missed the green grass and blue skies of the country, so she went back home.

❼ But she was glad she had brought her camera—the cows laughed with delight when they saw the pictures she took at the zoo!

HOW many nouns can you think of that begin with the first letter of your name? Make a list of people, animals, places, things, and feelings. Then use your words to write a story about yourself!

Chicken in the City

WRITTEN BY MARIA FLEMING
ILLUSTRATED BY KELLY KENNEDY

Be a Noun Detective: **Can you find the 16 nouns in this paragraph? Underline each noun you see. Then find the nouns in the word search puzzle. Answers can go across, down, or on a diagonal.**

A farm can be a very boring place for a chicken. What is there to do but look at the hay and talk to the cows? If you have a bored feathered friend on your hands, send her on an exciting trip to the fabulous Hen Hotel. She'll enjoy a beautiful view of the city from her own private nest, as well as delicious food from our famous menu—and we never, EVER, serve eggs!

This book has a lot of nouns in it. Do you know what a noun is? Share your ideas.

Lu-Lu the chicken lived on a farm,
but life in the country was losing its charm.

20
❶

Grammar Tales

A

F	X	T	R	I	P	W	Z	A
A	O	F	P	R	L	K	M	Q
R	T	O	R	H	A	Y	T	H
M	V	G	D	I	C	B	J	A
C	H	I	C	K	E	N	U	N
H	O	T	E	L	P	N	V	D
A	E	W	Z	W	E	Q	D	S
R	O	N	S	M	N	E	S	T
C	I	T	Y	X	E	G	G	S

㉑

silo   barn
tractor
cows
horse
pail
pigs
pond
ducks   mud

Day after day, Lu-Lu saw the same faces.

B

⑲

❷

A Box Full of Nouns:

Choose a noun from the box to complete each sentence. Then write your answers in the crossword puzzle.

Across

3. If you re feeling bored, you might need some

_____.

5. A _____ plows fields and bales hay.

6. If you re taking a trip, pack your _____.

8. You can buy a_____ from a street vendor.

9. Farm animals sleep in a_____.

Down

1. If you re tired of the city, you might go to the

_____.

2. If you don t want to walk, you can hail a _____.

4. You can see the city on a tour _____.

5. A chicken s skin is covered with _____.

7. You can see a show at the _____.

feathers	excitement	farmer
barn	taxi	country
suitcase	hot dog	theater
bus		

(18)

Nouns are words that name *people*, *animals*, *places*, and *things*. Look at the picture. Which nouns name people and animals? Which name places? Which name things?

She saw the same things. She saw the same places.

(3)

And she said to herself that night in her nest, "New can be nice. But old is the BEST!"

(16)

So she packed up her suitcase one day in the spring, and off Lu-Lu went with a wave of her wing.

(5)

Lu-Lu said to herself, "I need something new.
I'll move to the city—that's what I'll do!"

C

Let's Review: Nouns

A *noun* is a word that names a person, animal, place, or thing.

★ Some nouns name general people, animals, places, and things, like police officer, chicken, city, and suitcase.

★ A noun can also be a specific name, like Lu-Lu. This type of noun always begins with a capital letter.

★ Some nouns name things you can't see, hear, smell, taste, or touch. Excitement, charm, and life are nouns that name feelings and ideas.

★ How do you know if a word is a noun? Try putting a, an, or the in front of the word and using it in a sentence. Does it make sense? The chicken lived on a farm makes sense. Chicken and farm are both nouns.

In the city, Lu-Lu saw new things galore.

D

Look at the picture. How many nouns can you name? Remember, nouns name people, animals, places, and things. Can you come up with 15 nouns? Or 25 nouns? Or more? Make a list.

At the farm, Lu-Lu's friends held a big celebration and welcomed her back without hesitation.
Lu-Lu was happy to see all the old faces, all the old things, all the old places.

"I guess I'm just a country chicken at heart,"
Lu-Lu said to herself as she prepared to depart.
She repacked her bags and caught the next bus back home,
so she wouldn't have to spend her days all alone.

This page shows a lot of nouns that name things. Quick—look around your room. How many "naming nouns" can you list in two minutes?

She felt delight and excitement, wonder and awe at each new astonishing sight that she saw.

This page shows a lot of nouns that name places. Can you think of 10 more nouns that name places you might visit?

museum

zoo

amusement park

She visited places she'd never been before.

★★Swan Lake★

Some nouns name things you can't see or touch, like feelings or ideas. *Delight*, *excitement*, *wonder*, *awe*, *loneliness*, *life*, and *charm* are all nouns. Can you think of other nouns that name feelings or ideas?

But there was one other feeling Lu-Lu also detected.
A feeling this chicken hadn't expected . . .
loneliness. She missed her friends on the farm.
Now life in the city was losing its charm.

skater

musician

vendor

ICE CREAM

pigeons

dog

juggler

police officer

cyclist

cat

This page shows a lot of nouns that name people and animals. Can you think of nouns from A to Z that name people or animals?

For example, A is for *acrobat*; B is for *bug*; and so on.

She saw lots of new people and animals, too.

Even some of Lu-Lu's feelings were new.

Verbs

Background

A verb is a word that shows an action or a condition. There are several different types of verbs. Action verbs describe what someone or something does (*climb*, *juggle*, *swim*). Some action verbs describe activities you can't see or hear (*learn*, *imagine*, *find*). *Helping verbs* help the main verb describe present or future action (He *could* read; I *will* come back). Linking verbs describe a condition, or state of being (It *is* late; I *am* tired). Verbs can be in the present tense (*run*) or past tense (*danced*). Students will find several examples of each type of verb included in the story.

Before Reading

- Introduce the book to students with a discussion about their daily routines. Ask: *What is the first thing you do in the morning? How do you get to school each day? What are some things you do after school?* Encourage students to respond in complete sentences (I eat breakfast; I ride the bus; I play soccer) as you write their responses on the board. Then read the sentences together and invite students to tell which words describe their actions. As you help students find the verb in each sentence, explain that most verbs are words that tell what someone or something does. These are called action verbs.

- You can introduce the concept of linking verbs by asking questions such as: *How old are you?* or *What color is your shirt?* Again, write students' responses on the board in complete sentences (I *am* nine; It *is* red). Point out that some verbs do not describe an action—they describe a condition, or state of being. Explain that verbs like *am* and *is* are called *linking verbs*. They link the subject of the sentence to another noun or to an adjective.

- Next, show students the cover of the book and invite them to make predictions about the plot. What do they think the fairy will do for Herb? What are some actions that Herb might do in the story?

During Reading

After reading the story once through for meaning, you can reinforce a variety of concepts in subsequent readings.

- Invite students to raise their hands each time they hear an action verb.

- Help students distinguish between types of verbs by having them stand on action verbs and clap on linking verbs.

- Have students raise both hands when they hear a sentence that contains two verbs paired together, such as He *could run*. Challenge them to tell which is the main verb and which is the helping verb.

After Reading

In addition to the group overhead lesson and mini-book practice activities, try the following extensions to help reinforce students' learning.

- Play a game of verb charades. Write several action words on index cards (*fly*, *jump*, *swim*, *dance*, and so on) and place them in a paper bag. Invite students to take turns picking a card from the bag and pantomiming the verb for the group to guess. The first person to guess the correct verb performs the next action word.

- Sit students in a circle and challenge them to create a "verb chain." Begin the chain by saying a verb, such as *jump*. The student on your left must then say a verb that begins with the last letter of your verb (such as *play*). Continue around the circle as each student adds a verb to the chain (*yell*, *laugh*, *hang*, *grow*, and so on). Remind students that they can use linking and helping verbs as well (*would*, *did*, *does*, *should*). If anyone says a word that is not a verb, the chain is "broken" and the next player begins a new chain.

- You can turn the above idea into a written activity by having students write their verbs on short sentence strips. They can roll the strips into circles and link them together to form a paper chain. Hang the chain across a wall of the classroom for a unique twist on a word wall display. Then invite students to use the words to write action-packed stories.

To Extend Learning

Use the activity on the next page to reinforce and extend the concepts students have learned. You can turn this into a collaborative class activity by using the page on an overhead projector, or make multiple copies for students to work on individually.

- Have students read the directions at the top of the sheet. Then have them find the verb (or verbs) in each sentence.

- Invite students to take turns marking the verbs as directed, indicating which verbs show an *action* and which show a *condition*. Reinforce the terms *action verbs* and *linking verb*s by having students tally how many of each type they find.

Where's the Action?

Verbs

A verb can describe either an action or a condition. Verbs that describe actions are called *action verbs*. Verbs that describe conditions are called *linking verbs*.

> **Find the verb (or verbs) in each sentence.**
> - Underline the verbs that describe an action.
> - Circle the verbs that describe a condition, or state of being.

❶ Herb was very bored.

❷ He sat in a chair all day long, feeling blue.

❸ At last, a fairy flew through the window.

❹ "You are quite a sorry sight," she said.

❺ But she knew just what Herb needed.

❻ She pulled a verb out of her sack, and Herb was ready for action!

❼ He painted beautiful pictures and wrote amazing stories.

❽ After a lot of running and jumping, Herb was all tired out.

❾ So he crawled into bed with a book—his new favorite is the dictionary!

Take another look at the sentences above. Make a tick mark in the chart for each action verb and each linking verb you find. How many of each type did you find all together?

Action Verb	Linking Verb

Try This!

Would you rather read a good book or kick a soccer ball around? Make a list of action words that describe your favorite activities. Then compare lists with a friend. What hobbies do you have in common? It might be time to plan an action-packed day together!

A Verb for Herb

BY MARIA FLEMING
ILLUSTRATED BY KELLY KENNEDY

We're Going on a Verb Hunt: Can you find the 14 verbs in this paragraph? Look for action verbs, linking verbs, and helping verbs. Underline each verb you see. Then find the verbs in the word search puzzle. Answers can go across, down, or on a diagonal.

If you are bored, go on a Verb Vacation. Our expert tour guides will lead you all around beautiful Verb Village. Here you can find plenty of action—just drive around town in one of our Action Verb Autos, or see the sights from the Helping Verb Helicopter. You might even swim in the cool waters of Linking Verb Lake. And when it is time to leave, be sure to take home a souvenir dictionary as our free gift!

Herb was bored.
Herb was blue.
He sighed to himself,
"There's nothing to do."

Grammar Tales

A

```
A R E L T B U G O
X S W I M R E F Q
W T N S P V G C H
I P M W Z X D A G
L C N I K F I N D
L E A D G J U V R
Y H A Q V H S R I
S E E V Z C T K V
P N Y D E T A K E
```

zoom

㉑

What is a verb?
Most verbs are action words. They tell you what someone or something does. *Walk*, *shout*, *fly*, *listen*, and *sleep* are all action verbs. Can you think of others?

Along came a fairy.
She said, "Listen, Herb.
There's plenty to do.
All you need is a verb."

B

②

⑲

Help Wanted!

Choose a helping verb from the box to complete each sentence. Then write your answers in the crossword puzzle.

Across

2. Next, I think I _____ learn how to juggle, Herb said.

6. Visions of verbs _____ dancing in Herb's head as he fell asleep.

7. If you need a verb, you _____ look one up in the dictionary, the fairy told Herb.

Down

1. Now that I have verbs, I _____ going to run in the school race, Herb announced.

3. A fairy _____ flying through the window right now! Herb cried.

4. I _____ always wanted to learn magic, Herb said.

5. These verbs sure _____ keeping me busy! Herb thought.

6. Herb _____ feeling bored when the fairy arrived.

8. Herb _____ never seen a fairy before.

9. I _____ need a verb, Herb thought.

did	should	is
am	were	have
are	was	had
might		

Then she opened a sack, and out some verbs flew. "Pick one," she said. "Better yet, pick a few."

As Herb fell asleep
that night in his bed,
visions of verbs
danced in his head.

There are 23 helping verbs. Each always appears with another verb. Try using some in sentences.

am	do	must
are	does	shall
be	had	should
been	has	was
being	have	were
can	is	will
could	may	would
did	might	

He could dance.
He could sing.

> **Some verbs are called *helping verbs*. They help the main verb describe the action:**
>
> He could *run*.
>
> *Run* is the main verb. *Could* is a helping verb.

The fairy was right!
Herb could do anything.
He could run. He could jump.

C

Let's Review: Verbs

A *verb* is a word that shows an action or a condition.

★ Many verbs are action words. They describe what someone or something does. Climb, juggle, and swim are all action verbs. Remember, some action verbs describe activities you can't really see or hear. Learn, imagine, and find are all action verbs, too.

★ Some verbs help the main verb describe the action. These are called helping verbs. Could and will are examples of helping verbs: He could read. I will come back.

★ Some verbs are not action words. A linking verb describes a condition. Was and is are examples of linking verbs: Herb was bored. It is late.

★ How important are verbs? Just try writing a sentence without one! You cannot write a sentence without a verb. Verbs great! makes no sense. Verbs are great! makes sense because it includes the verb are.

He could swing, hit, slide,
score a home run,

D

> **Quick! How many verbs can you think of in one minute? Make a list.**

"So remember, next time
you need a distraction
just think of some verbs—
you'll be ready for action!"

"Dear boy," she chuckled,
"you don't need a fairy.
You can find verbs galore
in the dictionary."

ride a bike, climb a tree,
and juggle fruit just for fun.

Not all verbs are
action words.
Some verbs show
a condition. These
are called *linking
verbs*. They link
the subject of a
sentence to
another noun or to
an adjective:

Verbs *are* great.
I *am* tired.

"Wow!" said Herb.
"Verbs are great!
But I am tired,
and it is late."

pull rabbits from hats,
and disappear in a wink.

He could learn magic.
He could grow. He could shrink,

E

Here are some other linking verbs. Can you use them in sentences?

am	being	seem
are	feel	sound
be	is	was
been	look	were

Then Herb asked the fairy
as she packed up her sack,
"If I get bored again,
will you come back?"

He could read, write, dream,
imagine, explore,

F

swim, cook, paint,
and much, much more.

Adjectives

Background

An adjective is a word that modifies, or describes, a noun or a pronoun. Adjectives can tell how many (*many bugs*, *seven bugs*) or what kind (*long bug, green bug*). An adjective can describe any quality of the noun it modifies (*gigantic, sticky, friendly, surprised*). While many adjectives end in the letter *y* (*happy*, greedy), some adjectives can be formed by adding an ending such as *ic, ous, ish, ful, ing, al,* or *able* to a noun or verb (*fool+ish = foolish*). Sometimes a noun can become an adjective all by itself if it modifies another noun (*chocolate soda, kitchen sink*). As students will see in *The Bug Book*, adjectives serve to "dress up" nouns, making any piece of writing more descriptive and interesting.

Before Reading

- Introduce students to the importance of adjectives by writing a sentence without one. For instance, choose a student who is wearing a particularly colorful outfit and write the following sentence on the board: *Kayla is wearing a shirt.* Then ask volunteers to describe the article of clothing as you add their words to form a new sentence (*Kayla is wearing a red, striped, long-sleeved, fancy shirt.*). Point out each descriptive word and explain that these words are adjectives. An adjective is a word that modifies, or describes, a noun or a pronoun.

- Next, invite students to compare the two sentences. Which sentence helps students imagine the shirt more accurately? Explain that adjectives help readers form a "mental picture" of whatever is being described. You might also choose to point out that adjectives can be placed in different parts of a sentence. Sometimes adjectives appear right before the nouns they modify (*I saw a furry dog*), and sometimes they appear after a linking verb (*The dog was furry.*).

- Finally, show students the cover of the book and read the bugs' signs together. What other descriptive words might students use to describe each bug?

During Reading

After reading the story once through for meaning, you can reinforce a variety of concepts in subsequent readings.

- Invite students to clap once for each adjective they hear.

- Focus on common adjective endings by having students raise their hands only on adjectives that end in *ous*. Then try the same technique for *ic*, *y*, and so on.

After Reading

In addition to the group overhead lesson and mini-book practice activities, try the following extensions to help reinforce students' learning.

- Invite students to create "mystery bags." Provide each student with a paper bag and a secret small object such as a coin, button, rubber ball, and so on. Have students write a list of at least four adjectives on the outside of their bag to describe the object. Then have them place the object inside the bag and close it. Let each student present their mystery bag to the class, inviting the group to guess the secret object based on the adjective clues. This is a great way to reinforce the importance of using specific adjectives.

- Invite students to become adjective advertisers. Divide the class into small groups and assign each a product to sell, such as cereal or a computer game. Then have each group design an advertisement using descriptive adjectives. Post the advertisements on a bulletin board and discuss the effectiveness of each one. Which products look most appealing? Which would students want to buy? Point out that using vivid adjectives (*enormous*), as opposed to vague adjectives (*big*) can make students' writing more effective and engaging.

To Extend Learning

Use the activity on the next page to reinforce and extend the concepts students have learned. You can turn this into a collaborative class activity by using the page on an overhead projector, or make multiple copies for students to work on individually.

- Have students read the directions before each set of sentences. Invite volunteers to underline each adjective in the first section. Help students analyze the sentences in the second section to find the nouns being modified.

- Then invite students to practice using their own adjectives by rewriting the sentences at the bottom of the page.

Adjectives All Around

An adjective is a word that modifies, or describes, a noun or a pronoun.

Read the sentences below. Underline each adjective you see.

❶ Ten enthusiastic bugs decided to throw a wild party.

❷ They decorated their tiny house with long, colorful streamers.

❸ They invited many friends—big bugs, small bugs, short bugs, and tall bugs.

❹ They wanted to be friendly hosts, so they even made the grouchy bugs feel welcome.

Read the sentences below. Circle the noun that each underlined adjective modifies.

❺ When they brought out the <u>giant</u> cake, all the bugs were happily surprised.

❻ The ladybugs were especially <u>pleased</u>, because it was covered with red icing and black chocolate chip dots!

❼ Zany insects love <u>wacky</u> parties!

Read the sentences below. Sound boring? Add adjectives to each sentence to make it more detailed and interesting. Write your new sentence on the line.

❽ The bugs played music.

_____

❾ The centipede wore shoes.

_____

❿ The beetle spilled a drink on the rug.

_____

Which adjectives best describe you? Write an acrostic poem about yourself! Write the letters of your name down the left side of a sheet of paper. Then write an adjective beginning with each letter that describes something special about you.

Go Buggy! Can you find the 14 adjectives in this paragraph? Underline each adjective you see. Then find the adjectives in the word search puzzle. Answers can go across, down, or on a diagonal.

Do you know a special bug who could use a good time? Then call Caterpillar Caterers and let us help you plan a buggy bash! We have everything you need to throw a fabulous party for your favorite insect. We carry a complete line of party decorations to make your celebration festive. Choose from our many floral arrangements, which also make a delicious snack for hungry butterflies! So surprise the lovable larva in your life with a spectacular shindig today!

The Bug Book

BY MARIA FLEMING
ILLUSTRATED BY GARY SWIFT

Do you know what an adjective is? Share your ideas.

Adjectives are AWESOME!
There's just no doubt about it.
They take a noun—any noun—
and tell us more about it.
These bugs will demonstrate for you
just what an adjective can do.

```
S P E C I A L X Z Q P
F P F A V O R I T E H
A F E S T I V E G F J
B U Z C O M P L E T E
U Q F Y T K V W D C M
L X L O V A B L E V A
O G O O D Q C B K K N
U J R P C V B U G G Y
S P A R T Y X E L J T
D E L I C I O U S A K
F Z H U N G R Y D W R
```

㉑

Grammar Tales

A

clean bug

mean bug

An adjective is a word that describes a noun such as a bug. *Clean* **and** *mean* **are both adjectives.**

②

B

⑲

Rhyme Time: Make the adjectives rhyme with nouns they modify. Choose an adjective from the box to complete each clue. Then write your answers in the crossword puzzle.

Across

1. A comfortable insect is a _____ bug.

4. An unusual fruit is a _____ pear.

5. A heroic rescue is a _____ save.

6. A skinny smile is a _____ grin.

8. A joyful dog is a _____ collie.

10. An unruly tot is a _____ child.

11. A frightening sprite is a _____ fairy.

Down

2. A happy young man is a _____ lad.

3. A beautiful town is a _____ city.

7. An unfamiliar animal park is a _____ zoo.

9. An escaped bird is a _____ goose.

12. A scarlet mattress is a _____ bed.

brave	red	pretty
jolly	loose	wild
scary	thin	snug
rare	new	glad

Can you think of some other adjectives that describe these bugs?

gigantic, friendly, green bug

When you want to modify a noun,
an adjective won't let you down.
Try adding adjectives—they're incredible
at making nouns UNFORGETTABLE!

annoying, tagalong bug

18

3

16

5

strong bug

long bug

Let's Review: Adjectives

An *adjective* is a word that modifies, or describes, a noun or a pronoun.

★ Adjectives give more information about a noun. They can tell you how many (some bugs, seven bugs) or what kind (long bug, green bug). An adjective can tell you what someone or something looks like (gigantic), feels like (sticky), or acts like (friendly). An adjective can describe any quality of the noun it modifies.

★ Lots of adjectives have common endings. Many end in the letter y (pretty, happy, greedy). Sometimes you can make an adjective out of a noun or a verb by adding an ending such as -ic, -ous, -ish, -ful, -ing, -al, or -able. For instance, someone who acts like a fool might be described as foolish.

★ Sometimes a word that looks like a noun is really an adjective. For instance, a tagalong is someone who follows someone else. But in the phrase tagalong bug, the word tagalong describes the bug. That makes it an adjective. Other examples of adjectives "disguised" as nouns are chocolate soda and kitchen sink.

★ You can always tell that a word is an adjective if it tells you more about the noun it modifies.

sticky bug

picky bug

> **Can you think of adjectives to describe each of these bugs?**

many enthusiastic bugs

speedy bug

greedy bug

Lots of adjectives end in the letter *y*. How many can you think of?

gymnastic bugs

Sometimes you can make an adjective out of a noun or verb by adding a special ending such as *-ic*, *-ous*, *-ish*, *-ful*, *-ing*, *-al*, or *-able*.

Example:
hero + ic = heroic
courage + ous = courageous

Try to make adjectives out of these words:
humor, beauty, love, fool, magic, forget, wish, frighten

heroic and courageous bug

outrageous
bug

contagious bug

elastic bugs

silly bug

surprised
bug

chilly bug

disguised bug

Adverbs

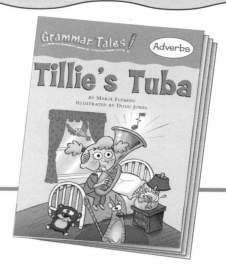

Grammar Tales!
Adverbs

Tillie's Tuba

BY MARIA FLEMING
ILLUSTRATED BY DOUG JONES

Background

An adverb is a word that modifies, or tells more about, a verb, an adjective, or another adverb. When an adverb modifies a verb, it can tell how (She plays *loudly*), when (She plays *early*), where (She plays *outside*), or to what extent (Her head hurt *tremendously*.). When an adverb modifies an adjective or another adverb, it often tells *how* or *how much* (The noise was *quite* horrendous; She plays *very* loudly). It is a common misconception that all adverbs end in –ly. Although many do (*proudly*, *enthusiastically*, *totally*), many others do not (*today*, *inside*, *never*). Adverbs can be a tricky concept: the only surefire way to tell if a word is an adverb is to figure out which part of speech it modifies in a sentence. Reading *Tillie's Tuba* will give students concrete practice in recognizing—and using—adverbs.

Before Reading

- Introduce the concept by asking students to name some of their favorite sports or activities. Write their responses on the board in noun-verb sentence form (*Carlos runs*). Then ask students to describe how they do their activity. Add an appropriate adverb to each sentence (*Carlos runs fast*). Explain that an adverb can tell more about a verb by describing how the action is done. After discussing a few examples, tell students that adverbs can also tell where and when something is done: *Carlos runs outdoors*; *Carlos ran yesterday*. Point out that an adverb can also tell *how* much: *Carlos runs often*.

- Then write a few examples of sentences in which the adverb modifies an adjective or another adverb. For instance: *Carlos was extremely happy when he won the race*; *Carlos runs very quickly*. Explain that a word is an adverb if it modifies, or tells more about, a verb, an adjective, or another adverb.

- Next, show students the cover of *Tillie's Tuba* and invite them to make predictions: how do they think Tillie will play her tuba? *When*, *where*, and *how often* will she play it? List students' suggestions on the board. Later, check to see how many of their adverbs appeared in the story.

During Reading

After reading the story once through for meaning, you can reinforce a variety of concepts in subsequent readings.

- Invite students to raise their hands each time they hear an adverb.

- Help students distinguish the different kinds of information adverbs can provide by having them raise their hands only when they hear an adverb that answers the question *How?* Then have them do the same for *where* and *when*.

- Reinforce the idea that not all adverbs have the *–ly* ending. Have students clap their hands for each adverb they hear that does not end in *–ly*.

After Reading

In addition to the group overhead lesson and mini-book practice activities, try the following extensions to help reinforce students' learning.

- Help students learn more about how adverbs modify with a fun twist on a charades game. Have each student write one verb (such as *sing*) and one adverb (such as *softly*) on separate index cards. When students are finished, collect the verb cards and place them in a bag. Place all the adverb cards in a separate bag. Then invite a child to choose one card from each bag. First, the student acts out the verb alone by pantomiming the action. Once the group has guessed the correct verb, the student then adds the adverb to the pantomime by doing the action in the appropriate manner. Students may find themselves acting out some very silly combinations! Once the group has guessed the correct verb and adverb (or appropriate synonyms), invite a new volunteer to perform the next pantomime.

- News reports are perfect for practicing adverbs because they naturally answer the questions *When? Where? How?* and *To What Extent?* Divide the class into small groups and assign each an event to report on, such as a fire or a town parade. Challenge groups to write a news article using adverbs to answer each journalistic question. You might invite group members to take turns reading their stories aloud in a "live broadcast."

To Extend Learning

Use the activity on the next page to reinforce and extend the concepts students have learned. You can turn this into a collaborative class activity by using the page on an overhead projector, or make multiple copies for students to work on individually.

- Read the directions at the top of the sheet. Help students distinguish between adverbs that tell how, when, where, and to what extent as you invite volunteers to mark up each sentence as indicated.

- For the second set of sentences, help students identify the word being modified by each adverb. You might also challenge them to name the part of speech.

- Then challenge students to turn adjectives into adverbs by rewriting the sentences at the bottom of the sheet.

Adverb Adventures

Adverbs

An adverb is a word that modifies, or tells more about, a verb, an adjective, or another adverb. An adverb can tell you how, when, where, or to what extent.

Find the adverbs in the sentences below.
- Underline the adverbs that tell you how.
- Circle the adverbs that tell you when.
- Draw a box around the adverbs that tell you where.
- Draw two lines under the adverbs that tell you to what extent.

❶ Tillie plays her tuba very loudly.

❷ Yesterday, she took her tuba outside and performed enthusiastically for the birds.

❸ But the birds found the noise really annoying, so they asked her to kindly cut it out.

❹ Tillie was extremely insulted and tearfully put her tuba away.

Read the sentences below. Circle the word that the underlined adverb modifies.

❺ "I'll play a concert for my goldfish!" Tillie thought <u>excitedly</u>.

❻ But the goldfish thought the concert was <u>completely</u> awful.

❼ "The violin might be <u>far</u> less annoying," he suggested.

Read the sentences below. Rewrite each sentence so it contains at least one adverb. Write your new sentence on the line.

❽ Tillie played her tuba with pride.

_____

❾ She practiced on it without end.

_____

❿ But she was happy to switch to the violin.

_____

Write a sentence about yourself describing something you do and how you do it. Use your name, a verb, and an adverb—and make sure all three start with the same letter. For instance: Susan sings softly. William walks willingly. Try writing sentences about your friends, too.

How's That? Can you find the 14 adverbs in this paragraph? Underline each adverb you see. Then find the adverbs in the word search puzzle. Answers can go across, down, or on a diagonal.

Do your neighbors complain **constantly** about your music practice? Do your friends run away when they see you open your tuba case? Or are you **simply** tired of playing the tuba **terribly**? If you're practicing **endlessly** but getting **nowhere**, don't despair—call Tuba Tutors **today**! Our professional music teachers will **patiently** guide you on your way to becoming a terrific tuba player. With our help, you can **soon** be marching **proudly** with the band or **sweetly** serenading your family to sleep. Don't delay—if you act **now**, we'll give you a brand new set of earplugs **absolutely** free! (Practice makes perfect, but it should **never** be painful!)

Tillie's Tuba

BY MARIA FLEMING
ILLUSTRATED BY DOUG JONES

This book has a lot of adverbs in it. Do you know what an adverb is? Share your ideas.

Tillie has a tuba.
She plays her tuba **proudly**.

Grammar Tales

A

```
C X P Z N E V E R U D
N O W H E R E G K E A
T S N V W J X F M N B
E O W S I M P L Y D S
R O B E T O D A Y L O
R N K F E A B J Q E L
I G Z H L T N U Z S U
B K C N P V L T W S T
L P R O U D L Y L L E
Y X A W A Y Q B P Y L
P A T I E N T L Y C Y
```

㉑

She plays **enthusiastically**.

B

⑲

❷

Adverbs Attack!

This puzzle is full of opposing adverbs. Complete each clue with the opposite of the underlined adverb. Then write your answers in the crossword puzzle. Hint: The missing word in each across clue appears in a down clue. You can match up pairs of clues to help solve the puzzle. Every underlined word appears once in the grid.

Across

2. The opposite of early is _____.

6. The opposite of slowly is _____.

7. The opposite of never is _____.

9. The opposite of outside is _____.

11. The opposite of far is _____.

12. The opposite of here is _____.

Down

1. The opposite of near is _____.

3. The opposite of late is _____.

4. The opposite of quickly is _____.

5. The opposite of inside is _____.

8. The opposite of always is _____.

10. The opposite of there is _____.

An adverb is a part of speech that modifies (tells you more about) a verb, adjective, or another adverb. Some adverbs tell you *how* something is done.

She plays her tuba **LOUDLY**.

Now she plays the violin!

She plays **early**. She plays **late**.
It fills her with delight.

> **Some adverbs tell you *when* something is done.**

Tillie loves her tuba.
She plays it **day** and **night**.

C

Let's Review: Adverbs

An *adverb* is a word that modifies— or tells you more about—a verb, an adjective, or another adverb.

★ When an adverb modifies a verb, it can tell you *how* something is done (She plays *loudly*), *when* something is done (She plays *early*), or *where* something is done (She plays *outside*). An adverb can also answer the question "To what extent?" (Her head hurt *tremendously*.)

★ When an adverb modifies an adjective or another adverb, it often tells you *how* or *how much* (The noise was *quite* horrendous. She plays *very* loudly).

★ Although many adverbs end in *-ly* (*proudly*, *enthusiastically*, *totally*), it's important to remember that many do not. Words like *today*, *inside*, and *never* are all adverbs, too.

★ The best way to tell if a word is an adverb is to figure out which word it modifies in a sentence. Ask yourself: *Does this word tell me more about a verb*, *an adjective*, *or another adverb*? If the answer is *yes*, it's an adverb!

She plays **anywhere** and **everywhere**—

D

Tillie kept her promise,
but her family just can't win.
Today she sold her tuba.

DON'S MUSIC STORE

This sentence is bursting with adverbs! Try writing a sentence that has as many (or more!) adverbs in it.

Tearfully, poor Tillie put **away** her tuba, then vowed **absolutely**, **positively** to **never** play **again**.

Tillie you can't play that tuba *here*.

Math Chapter7

Some adverbs tell you *where* something is done.

at home, at school, in town.

Finally, Tillie's family said, "**Kindly** take a break.

Adverbs can also answer the question "*To what extent?*"

Tillie thinks her tuba sounds **totally** stupendous. But her friends and family all agree the noise is **quite** horrendous.

She plays **inside**. She plays **outside**,
marching **up** and **down**.

E

Our heads all hurt **tremendously**.
Our ears **completely** ache."

When people see her coming,
they **quickly** run **away**.

F

It's **really** much **too** painful
to listen to her play.

What parts of speech do the
adverbs on these pages modify?
(Hint: Adverbs can modify verbs,
adjectives, or other adverbs.)

Pronouns

Background

A pronoun is a word that is used in place of a noun. There are several types of pronouns. The most common are *personal pronouns*, which name people or things. Just like nouns, pronouns can be singular (*I, me, you, he, she, him, her, it*) or plural (*we, us, you, they, them*). Pronouns that show ownership are called possessive pronouns (*my, your, our, his, hers, its, their*). Some pronouns can be used as subjects of sentences (*I, we, you, he, she, it, they*), while others are used as objects (*me, us, you, him, her, it, them*). Pronouns can make sentences simpler and help avoid repetition by standing in for nouns. The noun for which a pronoun stands is called its antecedent. *The Planet Without Pronouns* shows students just how important pronouns are— and how different our language would be without them!

Before Reading

- Introduce pronouns by inviting a volunteer to describe something he or she did last night (pronouns will naturally be included in students' descriptions). Write the volunteer's response on the board using complete sentences. Then underline any pronouns the student used, for instance: *I* watched *my* favorite TV show. *It* is about a superhero. *He* has special powers. Point out the pronouns to students and explain that a pronoun is a word that replaces a noun. Pronouns make sentences simpler and less repetitive. To illustrate, rewrite the description using no pronouns, for instance: Shayla watched Shayla's favorite TV show… and so on. Which description sounds better to students?

- Provide students with examples of different kinds of pronouns and help them distinguish between singular, plural, and possessive forms. Use sentences that provide personal context for students, for instance: Kate and Jesse play basketball. *They practice every day with **their** coach. **He** hopes the team will make the playoffs.* You might also choose to point out the difference between subjective and objective pronouns and give examples of proper usage, for instance: *I love basketball. It is very important to **me**.*

- Next, show students the cover of the book and invite them to make predictions about the story. How would a planet without pronouns be different from our planet? Can students find any clues in the cover illustration?

During Reading

After reading the story once through for meaning, you can reinforce a variety of concepts in subsequent readings.

- Invite students to raise their hands each time they hear a pronoun.

- Help students distinguish between different types of pronouns. They can clap their hands once for singulars and twice for plurals. Have students stand up each time they hear a possessive pronoun.

- As students find pronouns, stop occasionally and challenge them to locate the antecedent (the noun that the pronoun is replacing).

After Reading

In addition to the group overhead lesson and mini-book practice activities, try the following extensions to help reinforce students' learning.

- Invite students to create "pronoun people riddles." Challenge them to describe a person or a fictional character without using names—only pronouns. For instance: *She traveled from Kansas to Oz. Her house landed on a wicked witch.* The student who guesses the correct name (in this case, *Dorothy* from *The Wizard of Oz*) gets to make up the next riddle.

- Give students practice in substituting pronouns for nouns with this game. Write a variety of nouns on small slips of paper and place them in a paper bag. (Be sure to include both singular and plural nouns, as well as students' names.) Have students take turns picking two random nouns from the bag and using them in a sentence. Then challenge students to reword the sentence using the correct pronouns.

To Extend Learning

Use the activity on the next page to reinforce and extend the concepts students have learned. You can turn this into a collaborative class activity by using the page on an overhead projector, or make multiple copies for students to work on individually.

- Have students read the directions at the top of the sheet. Help them find the pronouns in each sentence and mark them as directed to indicate singulars, plurals, and possessives.

- Use the next set of sentences to help students identify the underlined pronoun's antecedent.

Super Stand-Ins

Pronouns

A pronoun is a word that "stands in" for a noun. Many pronouns name people or things. Some pronouns also show ownership.

> Find the pronouns in each sentence.
> - Circle the pronouns that name one person or thing.
> - Draw a box around the pronouns that name more than one person or thing.
> - Underline the pronouns that show ownership.

❶ Stanley built his own spaceship and rode it to a distant planet.

❷ He decided to explore Krimular and see what it was like.

❸ He met some friendly aliens, but he found them very strange.

❹ Their sentences were so long and complicated that he could barely understand them.

❺ "I know what's wrong!" he cried. "You don't use pronouns!"

❻ "I will teach you how to make sentences shorter," he told Zik.

❼ "My friends and I would love to learn," Zik replied.

Read each sentence below. Circle the noun that the underlined pronoun is standing in for.

❽ As he began his lesson, Stanley told the aliens that <u>they</u> needed to pay attention.

❾ So the aliens gathered around the blackboard, but they were so excited that they almost knocked <u>it</u> over.

❿ When the lesson was over, Stanley told the aliens that <u>he</u> had to go back home.

What would your neighborhood be like without pronouns? The next time you take a walk, look for pronouns on any signs or advertisements you see. Then rewrite the sign in your head without any pronouns. How would it look? Probably pretty silly—and a whole lot longer! It's much easier to say We Sell Fresh Fruit than The Owners of This Store Sell Fresh Fruit. Take a good look around you—you'll be glad you live on a planet with pronouns!

Pronouns on Parade: Can you find the 12 pronouns in this paragraph? Underline each pronoun you see. Then find the pronouns in the word search puzzle. Answers can go across, down, or on a diagonal.

Do your friends say you talk too much? Come to Pronoun Planet! We have plenty of pronouns in stock to help keep sentences short and sweet. Just listen to what our satisfied customers have to say:

"It used to take me hours to finish a sentence. Not anymore, thanks to Pronoun Planet!"
—Roberto Repetitive

"The people at Pronoun Planet were fantastic! They were so patient. I can't thank them enough!"
—Charlie Chatterbox

"Shorter sentences are mine!"
—Tina Talkative

People all over town are talking about Pronoun Planet—and finally, their friends have time to listen!

The Planet Without Pronouns

BY JUSTIN McCORY MARTIN
ILLUSTRATED BY JARED LEE

Welcome to Krimular

Stanley Sharpleton was an amazing kid! First, he built his very own spaceship. Then, he took it for a little spin. He zoomed past Jupiter and Saturn and Pluto. In fact, he kept right on rocketing until he reached a far-off purple planet called Krimular.

Grammar Tales

```
I X P L Q Z T V X
B Y O U R C H F S
Y A J I T K E G D
O G P N H B I C X
U L Z Q E V R F P
C B O Q Y F G M N
V X D U A W E K Y
M E F Z R L B C J
Z D X G Q T H E M
```

A

㉑

Stanley slipped on his gravity-defying sneakers and hurried down the space ladder. He'd done it! He'd landed on planet Krimular and he couldn't wait to explore.

B

②

---

he	him	they
their	it	she
her	me	his
your	our	

```
        ┌1┐   ┌2┬3┐
┌4┬─┬5┐ │ │   │ │ │
│ │ │ │ │ │   │ │ │
└─┴─┼6┼─┼─┼───┤ │ │
    │ │ │ │   └─┴─┘
┌7┐ └─┘ │ │
│ │     │ │
├8┼9┬─┬─┼─┤
│ │ │ │ │ │
└─┼─┼─┘ └─┘
  │ │
 ┌10┬─┐
 │ │ │
 └─┴─┘
```

⑲

Placing Pronouns

Choose a pronoun from the box to complete each sentence. Then write your answers in the crossword puzzle.

Across

2. Stanley climbed on _____ spaceship and headed back home.

4. Stanley liked the aliens even though _____ were strange.

6. "We thank you for visiting_____ planet," the aliens said.

8. Stanley taught the aliens how to keep _____ sentences simple.

10. "The spaceship belongs to _____," said Stanley.

Down

1. Stanley built a spaceship because _____ wanted to explore other planets.

2. Stanley called his mother because he didn't want _____ to worry.

3. Stanley was surprised when his sister said _____ had missed him.

5. If you don't use pronouns, _____ sentences will be too long.

7. Krimular looked strange to Stanley because _____ was so different from Earth.

9. Zik thanked Stanley for helping _____.

After walking a while, he reached a city. Aha! Just as he had suspected, there WAS life on Krimular! But something about this planet was very, very strange. Stanley just couldn't quite figure out what it was.

Go on a pronoun hunt! How many can you find in this story? When you're done, talk about everything you learned.

Back on Earth, Stanley got a call from Zik. "Is it all right if my family and I come for a visit?" he asked.

"Sure. You can stay in our guest room," said Stanley.

"Perfect," responded Zik. "Expect us Thursday—me, my parents, and my 2,978 brothers and sisters. I told them all about pronouns and they each want a lesson!"

Zam likes Zowie's new shoes!

Zowie likes Zam's new haircut!

Do you notice anything odd about how these two aliens address each other?

Stanley told Zik his name. "Zik is glad to meet Stanley," said Zik. "Stanley and Zik can be friends."

Suddenly Stanley felt a tap on his shoulder. He whirled around. "Greetings, Earthling," said a bright green creature with several arms. "Zik is named Zik. Tell Zik the name used to call the Earthling."

C

Let's Review: Pronouns

A *pronoun* is a word that is used in place of a noun. Many pronouns name people or things.

★ Some pronouns name one person or thing. For instance: *I love snow. It tastes good.* Other examples are *me, you, he, she, him,* and *her.*

★ Some pronouns name more than one person or thing. For instance: ***They** caught snowflakes. They enjoyed **them**.* Other examples are *we, us,* and *you.*

★ Some pronouns show ownership. For instance: ***Your** planet is amazing. Watermelon is **his** favorite flavor.* Other examples are *hers, its, ours,* and *theirs.*

★ Pronouns can make sentences simpler, shorter, and neater. They can also help you avoid repeating a word too many times. Which of these sentences sounds better?

    1. *Stanley caught a snowflake on Stanley's tongue and the snowflake tasted like watermelon.*

    2. *Stanley caught a snowflake on his tongue and it tasted like watermelon.*

★ The second sentence is much simpler. It uses the pronouns *his* and *it* in place of the words *Stanley's* and *snowflake.*

"Zik will show Stanley around Krimular," said Zik. "Look! Zik sees a Groogulak." Stanley looked where Zik pointed and saw a strange and beautiful animal. "Shhh," said Zik. "Stanley and Zik must not startle the Groogulak."

D

Next, Stanley gave Zik a farewell gift. It was his latest invention, an intergalactic cell phone. "This will help us keep in touch," he said.

"Wow! Thanks Stanley," replied Zik. "Correction: Thank you! I like it almost as much as I like pronouns."

Speaking, reading, and writing would be a lot harder without pronouns. What do you know about this important group of little words? Share your ideas.

At last, it was time for Stanley to return to Earth. "Thanks for teaching me all about pronouns. They sure come in handy," said Zik.

"Thanks for showing me all around Krimular. It's really out of this world!" exclaimed Stanley.

Suddenly, Stanley knew what was strange about Krimular. Zik didn't use pronouns. In fact, there were no pronouns to be found on the entire planet!

Important Pronouns

I
me
mine

it
its

he
him
his

you
yours

we
us
ours

they
them
theirs

she
her
hers

Some pronouns are used in place of people's names. These include *I*, *you*, *he*, and *she*.

A pronoun is a word that is used in place of a noun. Pronouns make sentences shorter and cut down on repetition.

Just then it started to snow, even though the weather was very warm. Zik darted about, catching the flakes in his mouth. "Zik loves snow. Correction: I love snow! Gee, pronouns do make things easier!"

When Zik nodded enthusiastically, Stanley pulled a collapsible space blackboard from his back pocket. "Pronouns are small words such as I, you, me, her, or them," explained Stanley. "They are used in place of nouns to make sentences simpler. Think of them as 'shortcut' words. For example, instead of saying, 'Zik sees a Groogulak,' you could say, 'I see it.'"

Stanley was happy to have met Zik. Without pronouns, though, it sure was going to be hard to communicate with his new friend. "Your planet is so amazing!" said Stanley. "But you could describe it even better if you used pronouns. Would you like to learn more about them?"

E

8

Stanley caught a flake on his tongue. It tasted like watermelon. He caught another. It tasted like a hot dog. He caught another. It tasted like pizza. "This one is the best!" he said.

Zik then replied, "Stanley's favorite flavor is pizza and so is Zik's. Correction: Your favorite flavor is pizza and so is mine."

13

When the lesson was done, Zik said, "I have processed the concept of pronouns and will master it shortly."

"Boy, you learn quickly!" replied Stanley.

"Not only do I have six hands, I also have six brains," remarked Zik. "Now, let's tour the rest of the planet."

F

10

Zik showed Stanley a huge volcano that spewed pink and green smoke and big bouncy balls with fancy patterns. "Take a look at the ballcano," said Zik. "The ballcano erupts every day. Correction: It erupts every day. I got so excited that I almost forgot to use pronouns."

11

Capitalization

Background

Capital letters are used to begin proper nouns—names of specific people, places, and things. Examples include: people's first, middle, and last names; cities, countries, and continents; days of the week, months, and holidays; historical periods and events; titles of books and movies; names of bands, sports teams, and magazines; and brand names of products. Whether or not a word is capitalized often depends on its function. If the word is functioning as a common noun (*I walked down the street*), it is not capitalized. If it is functioning as a proper noun (*I walked down Cherry Street*), it is capitalized. Capital letters are also used at the beginning of a sentence and in abbreviations (U.S.A.). The pronoun *I* is also always uppercase. *The Mega-Deluxe Capitalization Machine* provides plenty of examples to help students master the basic rules of capitalization.

Before Reading

- Introduce the topic by inviting volunteers to name their favorite books or movies. Write students' responses on the board using complete sentences—but without using any capital letters. For instance: *christina's favorite movie is robot wars.* Ask: *What is wrong with these sentences?* Work with students to correct each sentence. (You may wish to review capitalization rules for titles: explain that small words like *a*, *an*, *and*, *the*, and *of* are not capitalized unless they are the first or last words in a title.)

- Next, tell students the basic rule for capitalization: proper nouns are always capitalized. Explain that a common noun names a general person, place, or thing, while a proper noun names a specific person, place, or thing. Help students distinguish between common and proper nouns by providing examples of each, for instance: *chocolate chip cookies* and *Captain Cookie's Super-Crisps*.

- Then ask students to name any other places that need capital letters. Remind them that a capital letter is always used at the beginning of a sentence and that the pronoun I is also always capitalized. Capital letters are often used for abbreviations as well.

- Finally, show students the cover of the book and invite them to predict what the story might be about. What do they think the machine will do?

During Reading

After reading the story once through for meaning, you can reinforce a variety of concepts in subsequent readings.

- Have students raise their hands for each capitalized word they see in the illustrations. Then have them do the same for capitalized words in the body of the story.

- As students point out capitalized words, stop occasionally and challenge them to tell why the word is capitalized. Which capitalization rule is being applied?

After Reading

In addition to the group overhead lesson and mini-book practice activities, try the following extensions to help reinforce students' learning.

- Have a capitalization race. Make a deck of cards by writing each letter of the alphabet on a separate index card. Then shuffle the deck and have a volunteer choose a card at random. Set a timer and challenge students to list as many proper nouns as they can that begin with the chosen letter. Encourage students to include names of people, places, movies, books, sports teams, bands, and brand names of products. When the time is up, help students score their lists. Players receive one point for each properly capitalized word or phrase on the list.

- Invite students to become capitalization machines! Have students work in pairs: one partner "feeds" a slip of paper with a common noun to the partner playing the "machine." It is the machine's job to "transform" the common noun into a proper one. For instance, if a student receives the word *road*, he or she might write Lakeview Road on a new slip of paper and hand it back to the first student. After a few rounds, invite students to switch roles.

To Extend Learning

Use the activity on the next page to reinforce and extend the concepts students have learned. You can turn this into a collaborative class activity by using the page on an overhead projector, or make multiple copies for students to work on individually.

- Have students read the directions at the top of the sheet. Then read through the story, inviting students to point out any capitalization errors they see.

- Have students mark the errors as directed. You may also wish to have them rewrite the story on a separate sheet of paper using correct capitalization.

A Capital Caper

Names of specific people, places, and things begin with a capital letter. The beginning of a sentence is always capitalized. So is the pronoun *I*.

> The story below has 21 capitalization errors. Can you find them all?
> - Underline the uncapitalized words that SHOULD be capitalized.
> - Circle the capitalized words that should NOT be capitalized.

Cindy was running out of ideas for her science fair project. So far, she had tried out three different Inventions, and each one was a disaster! Her brother zeke thought she should invent a new kind of cereal. But when she tried out a box of garlic goodies on her family, nobody seemed to like them much. cindy's Father suggested she invent a robot to clean her room. But the robot kept misplacing things—Cindy still couldn't find her autographed copy of alien Adventures, and it was her favorite book! mrs. Cadoodle wanted Cindy to invent an automatic baseball pitcher. she thought it might help her favorite Team win the championship. But the manager of the springfield tigers said that only human players were allowed. "How will i ever come up with a new invention by next friday?" Cindy thought. Just then, she got a postcard in the mail from her friend lucy Lowercase, who had moved to louisiana in september. There were no capital letters in Lucy's note! The Postcard gave Cindy a wonderful idea. She got straight to work on her new machine—she knew she would amaze Mr. menlo and all the students at sunny street School!

Try This!

Write a paragraph about yourself including as many capitalized words as you can. You can include the name of your town and names of friends, family members, and pets. You can also include your favorite movies, books, bands, and sports teams. And don't forget your favorite holidays, snack foods, and toys! Check your work when you are finished. Did you capitalize correctly?

Grammar Tales — Capitalization

The Mega-Deluxe Capitalization Machine

BY JUSTIN McCORY MARTIN
ILLUSTRATED BY MATT PHILLIPS

7. ○ **S.** dina is getting a reporter from moxie magazine to cover the fair.
   ○ **T.** Dina is getting a reporter from Moxie Magazine to cover the fair.
   ○ **U.** Dina is getting a Reporter from Moxie magazine to cover the fair.

8. ○ **V.** The fair will be the biggest event that springfield has had in months.
   ○ **W.** The fair will be the biggest Event that Springfield has had in Months.
   ○ **X.** The fair will be the biggest event that Springfield has had in months.

9. ○ **Y.** It will be even more fun than last year's halloween parade.
   ○ **Z.** It will be even more fun than last year's Halloween parade.
   ○ **A.** It will be even more fun than Last Year's Halloween Parade.

The day of the science fair was finally here! And Cindy Cadoodle was ready. You see, she'd invented a great gadget and couldn't wait to show it off. It was called the Totally Terrific Turbo-Charged Mega-Deluxe Capitalization Machine.

20   **1**

A

10. ○ **B.** Just make sure to double-check the sign for your booth, because MR. Menlo is giving extra credit for good grammar!

 ○ **C.** Just make sure to double-check the sign for your booth, because Mr. Menlo is giving extra credit for good grammar!

 ○ **D.** Just make sure to double-check the sign for your booth, because Mr. Menlo is giving Extra Credit for Good Grammar!

Now crack the code! Each number below stands for one of the questions. Write the letter of the correct answer above each number. Then read your secret message!

You did a ___ ___ ___ ___ ___ ___ ___ job!
 10   1   6   3   7   1   4

"How does that contraption work?" Bonnie Brickle asked.

 "Allow me to demonstrate," said Cindy. She wrote Bonnie's name on a piece of paper.

 "That's wrong. You made it all lowercase!" exclaimed Bonnie.

B

4. ○ **J.** Olivia can't come to the fair because she'll be on vacation in hong kong.

 ○ **K.** Olivia can't come to the fair because she'll be on vacation in Hong kong.

 ○ **L.** Olivia can't come to the fair because she'll be on vacation in Hong Kong.

5. ○ **M.** Henry is doing a presentation on animals that lived during the ice age.

 ○ **N.** Henry is doing a presentation on animals that lived during the ice Age.

 ○ **O.** Henry is doing a presentation on animals that lived during the Ice Age.

6. ○ **P.** Freddie promised to bring enough Burpy Cola for everyone.

 ○ **Q.** Freddie promised to bring enough burpy cola for everyone.

 ○ **R.** Freddie promised to bring enough burpy Cola for everyone.

Capitalization Station: **Look at each set of sentences. Fill in the circle next to the sentence that uses correct capitalization. Then use the letters of your answers to decode the secret message at the end.**

1. ○ **A.** The school science fair is next Wednesday.
   ○ **B.** The school Science Fair is next wednesday.
   ○ **C.** The School science fair is next Wednesday.

2. ○ **D.** Cindy Cadoodle is working on a Secret Project.
   ○ **E.** Cindy cadoodle is working on a secret project.
   ○ **F.** Cindy Cadoodle is working on a secret project.

3. ○ **G.** I Heard That She's Making A Robot.
   ○ **H.** i heard that she's making a robot.
   ○ **I.** I heard that she's making a robot.

Rule #1:
People's first, middle, and last names always begin with capital letters.

"Just watch," responded Cindy. With that, she fed the paper into her invention. The machine bleeped and blipped and gurgled. Then out popped her name with the proper capitalization. "Wow!" screeched Bonnie. "Your invention really works!"

Remember to always capitalize . . .

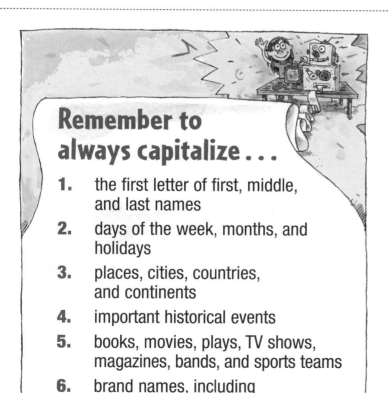

1. the first letter of first, middle, and last names
2. days of the week, months, and holidays
3. places, cities, countries, and continents
4. important historical events
5. books, movies, plays, TV shows, magazines, bands, and sports teams
6. brand names, including snacks and toys

Got it? Great. Now, brainstorm a list of words that fit in each category. Don't forget to capitalize them!

Rule #2:
Days of the week, months, and holidays are always capitalized.

The machine beeped and blared and chortled. Then out popped the words with the proper capitalization. "That's awesome!" exclaimed Gary.

"Let me try! Let me try!" shouted Gary Grigsby.

"Make sure you write in all lowercase," said Cindy. Gary wrote down his favorite month, day of the week, and holiday.

C

4

Let's Review: Capitalization

Capital letters are used to begin the names of specific people, places, and things.

★ Always capitalize the names of people (*Cindy Cadoodle*) and specific places (*Paris, France, Europe*).

★ Days of the week, months, and holidays also begin with capital letters (*December, Saturday, Halloween*). So do historical periods or events (*Renaissance, Civil War*).

★ Capitalize titles, too—whether it's the title of a book (*Barry Blotter and the Sorcerer's Soup*) or a movie (*Toy Tale*). The same rule applies to names of bands (*Sidestreet Guys*), plays (*The Longest Minute*), TV shows (*I Love Larry*), sports teams (*Florida Flyers*), and magazines (*Moxie Magazine*). Brand names also always begin with capital letters (*Chiperoos, Burpy Cola*).

★ How do you know when to capitalize a word? Here's a good rule to follow: If the word names something general (*the street*) you should not capitalize it. If the word is part of a specific name (*Cherry Street*), then it should be capitalized.

17

"My turn," said Olivia Orlando. Olivia was a world traveler. Her family always went on fantastic vacations. Olivia closed her eyes and thought about a place she dreamed of visiting. She wrote down the city, country, and even the continent.

D

6

The invention clanged and clapped and whistled. Then out popped the paper. On it, Mr. Menlo had written a single big, bold letter. It was Cindy's grade for the science fair project—an A+. Talk about a capital day!

15

Now it was the science teacher's turn to examine the machine. Cindy was very nervous. Mr. Menlo circled her invention, pushing buttons and twisting dials. After a few minutes, he announced: "Brilliant! Remarkable! Ingenious!" Then, quick as a wink, he jotted something on a piece of paper and fed it into the machine.

Rule #3:
The names of cities, countries, and continents always begin with capital letters.

Cindy's invention jumped and gibbered and yodeled. Then out popped the words with the proper capitalization. "Ooh-la-la!" remarked Olivia enthusiastically.

Freddie Farber loved ice cream. He also loved cookies, popcorn, lollipops, potato chips, beef jerky, soda, and bubble gum. Freddie wrote the names of his three favorite snacks in the whole world.

Rule #4:
Important historical events, such as the Boston Tea Party or Civil War, always begin with capital letters.

The machine sniffed and snorted and crackled. Then out popped the words with the proper capitalization. "Simply sensational," stated Henry.

Now it was Henry Hilbert's turn. Henry loved history. It was his favorite subject. He wrote down three fascinating historical events.

E

Rule #6:
Brand names of various items, such as snacks and toys, should be capitalized.

The machine gulped and gobbled and burped. Then out popped the words with the proper capitalization. "Mouthwatering!" cried Freddie.

"Don't forget me!" squealed Dina Duncan. Dina was always up on the latest trends. She wrote down her favorite book, movie, and rock band.

F

Rule #5:
The names of books, movies, and rock bands should be capitalized. The same goes for other kinds of entertainment such as plays, TV shows, magazines, and sports teams.

The invention rocked and rattled and clattered. Then out popped the words with the proper capitalization. "Utterly fabu!" declared Dina. "By the way, that's the newest way to say great."

Commas

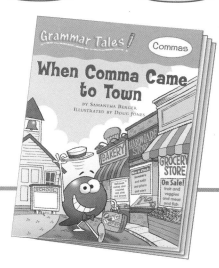

Background

Commas separate ideas and make a sentence's meaning clear. They are used to separate items, adjectives, or phrases in a series (*My favorite colors are blue, green, and red*). They are also used to separate clauses in a sentence (*As Sue sat down to eat, her dog took a bite*). Commas are used to set apart appositives, which are descriptive phrases that modify a noun (*Ned, my fish, is red*). They are also used after conjunctions *like*, *but*, or *yet* to separate the two parts of a compound sentence (*I like soccer, but I don't like baseball*). Commas in written language are parallel to pauses in spoken language: by slowing the reader down, they help clarify meaning. *When Comma Came to Town* provides concrete examples of the comma's many functions.

Before Reading

• Introduce the topic by asking a volunteer to name three or more favorite foods. Write the student's response on the board without using commas, for instance: *Jacob likes spaghetti ice cream cookies and soda.* Do students notice anything wrong with this sentence? Explain that commas are needed to separate each thing that Jacob likes. Without commas, the words run together and cause confusion. Does Jacob like spaghetti-flavored ice cream cookies? Work with students to insert commas in the correct locations. Explain that commas are used to separate items in a list of three or more.

• You can introduce use commas in compound sentences by asking your volunteer to a name a food he or she doesn't like. Write two sentences on the board, for instance: *Jacob likes spaghetti. He doesn't like broccoli.* Can students think of a way to combine these two ideas into one sentence? Write the following two examples on the board: *Jacob likes spaghetti, but he doesn't like broccoli. Jacob likes spaghetti but doesn't like broccoli.* Explain that both these sentences are correct, but only one needs a comma. How can students tell which is which? Teach them this trick: if they put their finger over the joining word (in this case, *but*), is there a complete sentence both in front of their finger and behind it? If the answer is yes, a comma is needed.

• Tell students that commas have additional uses that will be explored in the story. Show them the cover illustration and invite them to describe what is wrong with the signs. How will Comma help fix the problem?

During Reading

After reading the story once through for meaning, you can reinforce a variety of concepts in subsequent readings.

• Invite students to clap their hands once for each comma they see.

• Tell students to look carefully at the speech bubbles and signs in the illustrations. Help them identify the comma's different functions by having them clap their hands only on commas that separate items in a series, then only on commas that separate two parts (or clauses) of a sentence, and so on.

After Reading

In addition to the group overhead lesson and mini-book practice activities, try the following extensions to help reinforce students' learning.

• Divide the class into small groups and invite group members to survey one another on a given topic (such as favorite school subject areas). Then have them write the results of their survey in a sentence that uses commas to separate each piece of information, for instance: *Three people in our group like math best, two like science best, and one likes history best.*

• Invite students to create their own sentence-building puzzles. Give the group a topic to write about, such as pets. Have each student write a simple sentence on a sentence strip. For instance: *I like dogs; I don't like cats; I think hamsters make the best pets.* Prepare a set of comma cards by drawing a large comma on several index cards. Prepare a set of conjunction cards with words such as *but*, *so*, and *yet*. Then challenge students to combine their sentences by adding a comma and a conjunction, for instance: *I like dogs, but I think hamsters make the best pets.* How many sentences can they build that make logical sense?

To Extend Learning

Use the activity on the next page to reinforce and extend the concepts students have learned. You can turn this into a collaborative whole-class activity by using the page on an overhead projector, or make multiple copies for students to work on individually.

• Have students read the directions at the top of the sheet. Invite them to examine each sentence, adding any necessary commas and crossing out unnecessary ones.

• As students mark up the text, encourage them to explain their reasoning. Why are commas needed in some places and not in others?

Comma Conundrums

Commas

Commas are used to separate items or ideas in a sentence.

Read each sentence below.
- Write in any missing commas. • Cross out any unnecessary commas.

❶ Before Comma came to town people's sentences were very long.

❷ One boy told his friends, that his favorite ice cream flavors were, peach chocolate vanilla strawberry fudge-ripple and butterscotch.

❸ The town bakery sold, cakes cookies pies and bread.

❹ Comma thought, that the land of And was the nicest friendliest prettiest, place he'd ever seen.

❺ He knew he could help the townspeople although it would take a lot of work.

❻ The townspeople wanted to thank Comma so, they threw him a party.

❼ Comma wished he could stay, in the town forever but he had many other places, to visit.

❽ Ned the town fish sadly, waved, his fin goodbye.

❾ Comma wished all the townspeople, good luck good health and good grammar!

What's in your pockets right now?

What would you find if you emptied your backpack? Write a sentence listing the things you're carrying around with you today. Be sure to use commas in all the right places!

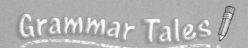

When Comma Came to Town

BY SAMANTHA BERGER
ILLUSTRATED BY DOUG JONES

7. ○ **S.** Comma could see that they were in trouble, so he promised to help them.

○ **T.** Comma could see that they were in trouble so, he promised, to help them.

○ **U.** Comma could see, that they were in trouble, so he promised to help them.

8. ○ **V.** He taught them how to make their sentences, neater shorter and cleaner.

○ **W.** He taught them how to make their sentences neater, shorter, and cleaner.

○ **X.** He taught them, how to make their sentences neater, shorter and cleaner.

9. ○ **Y.** Everyone was grateful especially the people, who worked at the sign factory!

○ **Z.** Everyone was grateful especially the people who worked at the sign factory!

○ **A.** Everyone was grateful, especially the people who worked at the sign factory!

Once upon a time, there was a place called And. It had the longest sentences in all the land.

Grammar Tales

A

Now crack the code! Each number below stands for one of the questions. Write the letter of the correct answer above each number. Then read your secret message!

Now you're using "comma __ __ __ __ __ !"

7 2 5 7 2

21

My favorite ice-cream flavors are chocolate **and** peach **and** mint **and** vanilla **and** fudge-ripple **and** strawberry **and** bubble gum **and** butterscotch.

Before

Every sentence was such a drama—
that is, until folks met the comma.

B

---

4. ○ **J.** The town which was small barely had room for its own signs!

   ○ **K.** The town, which was small, barely had room for its own signs!

   ○ **L.** The town which was small barely had room, for its own signs!

5. ○ **M.** The grocery store had the longest messiest sign he'd ever seen.

   ○ **N.** The grocery store had the longest, messiest sign he'd ever seen.

   ○ **O.** The grocery store, had the longest, messiest sign he'd ever seen.

6. ○ **P.** The people, were friendly and kind, but their sentences were endless.

   ○ **Q.** The people were friendly, and kind, but, their sentences were endless.

   ○ **R.** The people were friendly and kind, but their sentences were endless.

2

19

Look at each set of sentences. Fill in the circle next to the sentence that uses commas correctly. Then use the letters of your answers to decode the secret message at the end.

1. ○ **A.** Comma traveled over a bridge across a river and through the woods to get to town.

   ○ **B.** Comma traveled over a bridge, across a river, and through the woods to get to town.

   ○ **C.** Comma traveled, over a bridge, across a river and through the woods to get to, town.

2. ○ **D.** He stopped at a restaurant for a hamburger some fries and a shake.

   ○ **E.** He stopped at a restaurant for a hamburger, some fries, and a shake.

   ○ **F.** He stopped, at a restaurant, for a hamburger some fries and a shake.

3. ○ **G.** Finally, he arrived, in the town, of And.

   ○ **H.** Finally he arrived, in the town, of And.

   ○ **I.** Finally, he arrived in the town of And.

18

When your sentence has a list, you can put commas between each item instead of the word *and*. The sentence gets shorter and sounds better!

As soon as Comma came to town,
he took their sentences and cut them down.

3

"Safe trip! Thank you!" everyone cheered.
"We've learned so much since you've been here!"

16

On a separate sheet, shorten this sentence by replacing all but the last *and* with commas:

My favorite colors are blue and green and red and yellow and orange and purple and pink and periwinkle.

But with Comma around, it was easily seen,
you could take out the ands and put commas between.

5

Before that, lists went on and on—
and conversations made folks yawn!

C

Let's Review: Commas

Commas can help separate ideas and clear up the meaning of a sentence.

★ Commas are used to separate a list of items, adjectives, or phrases. For instance: *My favorite colors are blue, green, and red.*

★ Commas are also used to separate two parts of a sentence. This helps make the meaning of the sentence clear. For instance: *As Sue sat down to eat, her dog took a bite.* That sentence would be very confusing without the comma!

★ You can also use commas to make one sentence out of two shorter ones. For instance: *My fish is red. His name is Ned.* These ideas might be joined with commas to become: *Ned, my fish, is red.*

★ Words like *but* and *yet* are often used with a comma to join sentences. For instance: *I like soccer. I don't like baseball.* The joined sentence might read: *I like soccer, but I don't like baseball.*

★ How can you tell when you should use a comma? Remember that a comma is like a pause when someone is speaking. Try reading the sentence out loud. If a short pause makes sense, a comma probably will, too!

Next, Comma showed what he could do when perched beside an adjective or two.

D

Commas can often be found in sentences that have the words *but*, *yet*, and *although*. See if you can figure out where commas belong in these sentences:

1. She loves soccer but not as much as gymnastics.

2. He tried and tried yet he just couldn't hula-hoop.

3. I don't like broccoli although I do prefer it to asparagus.

The folks of And would miss Comma a lot.
Still, they'd never forget the lessons he taught.

There were other places he needed to go—
like But and Yet, not to mention Although.

With Comma's help, their sign looked neater—
crisper, cleaner, shorter, and sweeter!

On a separate sheet of paper, shorten the sentence by replacing all but one *and* with a comma.

We went on the Stupendo Slide and then we went on the Gigantor Swings and then we went on the Turbo Wheel and then we went on the Glow-Coaster!

Everything was easier to understand
when Comma came to the land of And!

Where do you think commas should go in this sentence?

Just before bed he took a bubble bath read a book and drank hot chocolate.

Do not panic! Do not fear!
One little comma makes it all clear:
As Sue sat down to eat, her dog took a bite.
He bit her burger? Now that sounds right!

Yet there was more that Comma could do.
He cleaned up confusing sentences, too:
As Sue sat down to eat her dog took a bite!
Sue ATE her dog?! That couldn't be right.

E

8

But then, one day, with a great big sigh,
it was time for Comma to say good-bye.

13

What's more, just by adding some curlicue dots,
Comma can join up two separate thoughts!
Instead of two sentences:
My fish is red. His name is Ned.

F

10

Can you combine these two sentences? (Hint: You'll need to add two commas and cut a few words.)

My gerbil is cute. Her name is Bertha.

There can be just one:
Ned, my fish, is red.

11

Quotation Marks

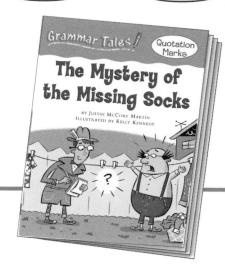

Grammar Tales!   Quotation Marks

The Mystery of the Missing Socks

BY JUSTIN McCORY MARTIN
ILLUSTRATED BY KELLY KENNEDY

Background

Quotation marks are used to show the exact words that someone says. They surround the speaker's words, appearing both before and after a direct quote: The boss said, *"Get the story."* The speech tag can appear before the quotation, as in the above example, or after the quotation: "Get the story," *said the boss.* In longer quotations, the speech tag can be placed in the middle: "I'd bet my hat," *said Mrs. Slice,* "that it was Harold." Like periods, question marks and exclamation points are placed inside the closing quotation marks if they are part of the quote: *"Can you believe it?" Mike asked. "I just saw Harold running through the park!" Jenny shouted.* Quotation marks are only used for direct quotes, never for summaries or paraphrases. Students will find examples of several quotation styles and their correct punctuation in *The Mystery of the Missing Socks.*

Before Reading

•Introduce the concept of direct quotations by eliciting simple statements from students. For instance, you might ask: *What are you doing after school today?* Then write a student's response on the board as both an indirect and a direct quotation. For instance: *Paulo said he has to go to the dentist; Paulo said, "I have to go to the dentist."* Point out the quotation marks in the second sentence and ask students if they know what these marks mean. Explain that they show exactly what a person says. Can students guess why you did not use quotation marks in the first sentence? Explain that the first sentence summarizes what Paulo said, but does *not* use his exact words. Quotation marks are used only for exact quotes.

•Use additional student responses to demonstrate the use of speech tags which is the part of the sentence that tells who is speaking. Give examples that appear before, after, and in the middle of quotes. You may also like to point out basic punctuation rules: quotation marks are used at the beginning and end of the speaker's words, a comma separates the quote from the speech tag, the quote begins with a capital letter (unless a sentence is being continued), and end punctuation is placed inside the closing quotation marks.

• Next, show students the cover of the book and invite them to make predictions about the story. Why might quotation marks be an important tool for a reporter?

During Reading

After reading the story once through for meaning, you can reinforce a variety of concepts in subsequent readings.

• Help students recognize quotations by inviting them to take turns speaking the characters' dialogue. Encourage them to use different voices for different characters.

• Invite students to raise their hands each time they see Steve write a direct quote in his notebook. For an additional challenge, you might stop and ask students to tell where the speech tag appears: before, after, or in the middle.

After Reading

In addition to the group overhead lesson and mini-book practice activities, try the following extensions to help reinforce students' learning.

• Students can practice dialogue conventions by rewriting comic strips. Provide students with several examples of simple comic strips that include speech balloons. Explain that in comics, the words inside a character's speech balloon represent a direct quote. Then challenge them to rewrite the story using quotation marks and correct punctuation.

• Invite students to become reporters like Steve Scoop. They can interview one another about a variety of topics, such as favorite activities or special talents. Challenge students to write an article based on their interview using at least two direct quotations. If available, you might even have students use a tape recorder for their interviews, and then choose the quotes they'd like to transcribe.

To Extend Learning

Use the activity on the next page to reinforce and extend the concepts students have learned. You can turn this into a collaborative class activity by using the page on an overhead projector, or make multiple copies for students to work on individually.

• Have students read the directions at the top of the sheet. Help them find the quote in each sentence and insert quotation marks in the correct locations.

• In the second set of sentences, have students check for correct quotation mark usage as well as correct punctuation. Invite them to insert quotation marks and commas where needed. Then help students rewrite the sentences at the bottom of the page, including quotation marks, commas, and proper capitalization.

Quotation Locations

Quotation marks show the exact words that someone says. Remember these rules:

- Quotation marks are placed before and after the speaker's words.
- Quotations begin with a capital letter unless they continue a sentence.
- A comma separates the quotation from the words that tell who is speaking.
- Periods are placed inside the ending quotation marks.
- If the speaker's words end with a question mark or an exclamation point, it is placed inside the ending quotation marks.

Read each sentence below. Insert quotation marks in the correct places.

❶ I need a report on Mr. McGillicutty's missing socks for tomorrow's paper, Steve's boss said.

❷ Don't worry, said Steve. I'm an expert on missing socks. I'll get right on it!

❸ Can you tell me exactly what your socks looked like? Steve asked Mr. McGillicutty.

❹ Mr. McGillicutty answered, They were extra large and had polka dots.

Read each sentence below. Insert any missing quotation marks. Insert any missing commas.

❺ "If anyone likes polka-dot socks, said Mrs. Slice, it's Harold."

❻ "That's true" Jenny Jennings said. "But Harold likes any kind of socks!

❼ Harold once tried to take my socks right off my feet" said Mike Montey.

❽ Arf, arf said Harold.

Try This!

Imagine that you are someone famous, and the newspaper wants to print a quote from you. What would you like to be known for having said? Write your quote as it would look in a newspaper article. If you like, you can even write a whole interview with yourself—but don't forget to use your quotation marks!

The Mystery of the Missing Socks

BY JUSTIN McCORY MARTIN
ILLUSTRATED BY KELLY KENNEDY

7. ○ **M.** Steve said, "What a hot story! Now all I need is a good ending."

 ○ **N.** Steve said, "What a hot story!" Now all I need is a good ending.

8. ○ **O.** "What do you have to say for yourself? he asked Harold."

 ○ **P.** "What do you have to say for yourself?" he asked Harold.

9. ○ **Q.** "Grrrr, Harold replied.

 ○ **R.** "Grrrr," Harold replied.

> **This book is about quotation marks. Do you ever use them in your writing? When?**

Hi! My name is Steve Scoop, and I'm a reporter for the Hoopletown Evening Herald. My job is to talk to people and write down what they say. I have three important tools: my notebook, my pencil, and quotation marks.

10. ○ **S.** "That's fascinating, said Steve." Can I quote you on that?

○ **T.** "That's fascinating," said Steve. "Can I quote you on that?"

Now crack the code! Each number below stands for one of the questions. Write the letter of the correct answer above each number. Then read your secret message!

You really ___ ___ ___   ___ ___ ___
            4   5   10   10   4   3

___ ___ ___ ___!
7   1   9   6

Grammar Tales

A

---

4. ○ **G.** "Yes!" Mr. McGillicutty cried. Just this morning!

○ **H.** "Yes!" Mr. McGillicutty cried. "Just this morning!"

5. ○ **I.** "I had a pair stolen last week," added Mrs. Slice.

○ **J.** "I had a pair stolen last week, added Mrs. Slice.

6. ○ **K.** "Look!" shouted Jenny Jennings. "Someone's stealing mine right now!"

○ **L.** "Look! shouted Jenny Jennings. "Someone's stealing mine right now!

I've just received a hot tip. Mr. McGillicutty is missing a pair of polka-dot socks. My boss wants me to write a story about it for the newspaper.

B

Quotation Marks Mark the Spot: Look at each set of sentences. Fill in the circle next to the sentence that uses quotation marks correctly. Then use the letters of your answers to decode the secret message at the end.

1. ○ **A.** "I've got a great idea for a story," Steve told his boss.
   ○ **B.** "I've got a great idea for a story, Steve told his boss."

2. ○ **C.** Okay, said his boss, "but make sure to get some good quotes."
   ○ **D.** "Okay," said his boss, "but make sure to get some good quotes."

3. ○ **E.** Steve asked Mr. McGillicutty, "Have you had any socks stolen recently?"
   ○ **F.** "Steve asked Mr. McGillicutty," Have you had any socks stolen recently?

Quotation marks surround a person's words. That way, you know exactly what he or she said.

See, I've written down what my boss said in my notebook. I used quotation marks. Don't they look like they've captured the words? That's what quotation marks do. They're used to show the exact words that someone said.

★ *Hoopletown* ★
EVENING HERALD
ALL THE QUOTES THAT ARE FIT TO PRINT 10¢

MISSING SOCK MYSTERY SOLVED

◎ ◎ BY STEVE SCOOP ◎

Harold

Mr. Clyde McGillicutty lost a pair of socks today. At approximately 9:00 AM he hung them on his clothesline to dry. Then, when he went out to get them at 11:30 AM, they had vanished. "My socks just disappeared!" exclaimed Mr. McGillicutty.

A neighbor, Ms. Enid Slice, suggested a likely sock-snatching suspect. "I'd bet my hat," she said, "that it was Harold."

Mr. Mike Montey, the mail carrier, agreed, saying that Harold often gives him trouble. "Can you believe Harold chased me down the street and helped himself to a bunch of letters?" asked Mr. Montey.

It was truly hard to believe. But this reporter was determined to find the footwear fiend. Jenny Jennings, age 10, provided a helpful clue. "I just saw Harold running toward the park!" she reported.

Upon arriving at the park, a pair of polka-dot socks was spotted lying on the ground. Nearby was a small dog. According to his tag, his name was Harold. Mystery solved. Asked what he had to say for himself, Harold replied, "Arf, arf."

In a late-breaking development, the socks have been returned to Mr. McGillicutty. He promptly put them on and is very happy.

Weather: Really Nice

I had better get to work. My first stop is the scene of the crime—Mr. McGillicutty's backyard.

Oops. My boss just told me to stop writing down every word she says.

C

Let's Review: Quotation Marks

Quotation marks are used to show the exact words that someone says.

★ Quotation marks surround the speaker's words. They always appear both before and after the quotation, for instance: *"Get the story," said the boss.*

★ The speaker's name can appear before a quotation: *Ms. Slice said, "I'd bet my hat that it was Harold."* It can appear after a quotation: *"I'd bet my hat that it was Harold," said Ms. Slice.* It can even appear in the middle: *"I'd bet my hat," said Ms. Slice, "that it was Harold."*

★ When the speaker is asking a question, the question mark goes inside the closing quotation marks: *"Can you believe Harold chased me down the street, then helped himself to a bunch of letters?" asked Mike Montey.* If the person is speaking loudly or excitedly, the same goes for an exclamation point: *"I just saw Harold running toward the park!" Jenny shouted.*

★ How do you know when to use quotation marks? Only use them if you are writing someone's exact words. For instance, this sentence does not need quotation marks: *Harold barked.* But this one does: *"Arf, arf," said Harold.* That's because *"Arf, arf"* is **exactly** what Harold said!

My socks just disappeared!

Mr. McGillicutty tells me that, around 9:00 AM, he hung his wash on the clothesline to dry. But when he went out to get it at 11:30 AM, his favorite pair of polka-dot socks had disappeared!

D

"Arf, arf," said Harold the dog.

> To keep your writing lively, it's a good idea to find other words to use in place of *said*. For example, you could substitute:
>
> - remarked
> - exclaimed
> - commented
> - shouted
> - screamed
>
> - laughed
> - reported
> - whispered
> - sighed
> - barked
>
> **Which one works best here? Can you think of some others? Brainstorm a list.**

Naturally, I wrote down Harold's statement. Looks like the case of Mr. McGillicutty's missing socks is officially closed. Now, I just have to write the story.

What have we here? There's a pair of polka-dot socks lying on the ground. They are right beside a dog. Let's see if I can make out the name on his tag … Just as I suspected: Harold! Looks like I located the polka-dot sock thief!

When you quote people, you have the choice of putting their name at the beginning, middle, or end of the sentence. This time Steve chose the end, but he could also have chosen the beginning or middle:

• Mr. McGillicutty said, "My socks just disappeared!" (beginning)

• "My socks," said Mr. McGillicutty, "just disappeared!" (middle)

See, I've written down exactly what Mr. McGillicutty said. I placed his comments inside quotation marks. I wonder if his neighbors noticed anything suspicious. I better go investigate.

Now I'm talking to a girl named Jenny Jennings. She's ten years old. Jenny says that, just a few minutes ago, she spotted Harold dashing toward the park.

Where did Steve place the speaker's name this time—at the beginning, middle, or end of the sentence?

I want to remember Ms. Slice's comment. So I wrote down exactly what she said. I've got to find out more about this mysterious Harold.

Now I'm talking to Ms. Slice. She's given me a really great tip.

E

Exclamation points are used in quotations when the speaker is talking either loudly or excitedly. Remember, exclamation points also go inside the closing quotation marks, the same as question marks.

Jenny gave me a really great lead. So I wrote it down. I'm hot on Harold's trail now!

Here's Mike Montey, the mail carrier. He knows the suspect all right, and has some pretty alarming things to say about him.

F

Question marks go inside of the closing quotation marks.

This is incredible! Boy, I wrote down every word. This Harold sounds like a real bully.

Sentence Structure

Background

One of the most common mistakes in sentence structure is the run-on sentence. A sentence is a group of words that expresses a complete thought or idea. A run-on sentence tries to carry too many ideas at once, making it "run on" way too long. Run-on sentences also occur when two or more ideas are linked together improperly, or without the correct punctuation. For instance: *The monster's name was Bernard, he had orange polka dots on his back.* Run-on sentences can be corrected by dividing the ideas into separate sentences (*The monster's name was Bernard. He had orange polka-dots on his back.*) or by adding a conjunction (*The monster's name was Bernard, and he had orange polka-dots on his back.*). If the ideas are closely related, a semicolon may also be used. *The No-Good, Rotten, Run-on Sentence* provides students with the tools they need to recognize—and correct—errors in sentence structure.

Before Reading

• Introduce the topic by providing students with the following definition: *A sentence is a group of words that expresses a complete thought or idea.* Based on this definition, can students guess what a run-on sentence is? Provide an example by inviting students to share their thoughts and ideas about a movie they've seen recently, or a book they've read. Then write a sentence on the board, stringing their ideas together to create a run-on. For instance: *The movie was good, it had great special effects, awesome costumes.* Ask: *How many different ideas can you find in this sentence?* Explain that this is a run-on sentence because all the ideas "run" together.

• Then work with students to correct the run-on by giving each idea its own sentence, for instance: *The movie was good. It had great special effects.* Explain that run-on sentences can also sometimes be corrected by adding a word such as *but, yet, for,* or *and: The movie had great special effects and awesome costumes.* Be sure to point out that run-on sentences don't have to be long: any sentence that improperly links two or more ideas is a run-on.

- Next, show students the cover of the book and invite them to make predictions about what happens when Kevin tries to write a story.

During Reading

After reading the story once through for meaning, you can reinforce a variety of concepts in subsequent readings.

- Invite students to follow Kevin's run-on sentence throughout the story illustrations. Challenge them to identify each separate thought or idea in the sentence.

- Challenge students to edit Kevin's run-on sentence as they read. Invite them to suggest places where a new sentence might begin, or where a connecting word might be added.

After Reading

In addition to the group overhead lesson and mini-book practice activities, try the following extensions to help reinforce students' learning.

- Help students "tame" their own no-good, rotten, run-on sentence. In advance, write an outrageously long run-on sentence on a roll of adding machine tape. Roll the tape back up and gather the group together. Tell them that you are about to unleash an out-of-control sentence, and that their job will be to make it more manageable by breaking it up. Provide students with scissors and pencils. Then let the roll unfurl across the floor and let students get to work!

- Reinforce the idea that a sentence need not be long to be a run-on. Write a short run-on sentence on the board, such as *I'm hungry, let's eat.* Invite students to explain why the sentence is a run-on (it improperly links two ideas) and suggest a way to correct it (break it into two sentences). Then invite students to work with a partner to see who can come up with the shortest run-on.

To Extend Learning

Use the activity on the next page to reinforce and extend the concepts students have learned. You can turn this into a collaborative class activity by using the page on an overhead projector, or make multiple copies for students to work on individually.

- Have students read the directions at the top of the sheet. Then have them read the story and identify the separate ideas in each sentence.

- Invite students to correct the run-ons by rewriting the story on the lines. They can create separate sentences by adding periods and capital letters. They can also make use of connecting words such as *but, yet, because,* or *and.*

Run-ons Run Wild!

A run-on sentence is a sentence that tries to carry way too many ideas. Run-on sentences are also caused by linking two or more ideas improperly, or without the correct punctuation.

The paragraph below is riddled with run-ons! Rewrite the story on the lines to correct the run-on sentences. Remember these tips:

- You can divide ideas into separate sentences by adding periods and capital letters.
- You can link ideas properly by using connecting words such as *but*, *yet*, *because*, or *and*.

Kevin Crabtree decided to write a new story, this one was about a monster named Gertrude the Gabber. No one listened to Gertrude at the Monster Meetings, she talked too much. Everyone said that her sentences went on and on there was just no stopping her! Then she met a monster named Edwin the Editor he told her all she needed was a pencil to shorten her sentences. Gertrude didn't believe him, she tried it at the next meeting. Now Gertrude is an excellent speaker, she's also the Monster Club's new secretary!

_____

_____

_____

_____

_____

_____

Try This!

Kevin's story had a lot of good ideas, but they were all crowded into one sentence. You can write your own no-good, rotten, run-on sentence and then fix it yourself! Just let your ideas flow out on the paper. Don't worry about punctuation. Then go back and fix your story by breaking it into separate sentences and adding correct punctuation. Which version looks better?

8. ○ **O.** Miss Bartlebine gave Kevin her pencil and showed him how to fix the problem.

   ○ **P.** Miss Bartlebine gave Kevin her pencil, she showed him how to fix the problem.

9. ○ **Q.** Running all over town Kevin discovered a new talent.

   ○ **R.** After running all over town, Kevin discovered a new talent.

10. ○ **S.** Not only was he a good writer he was also a fast runner.

    ○ **T.** Not only was he a good writer, but he was also a fast runner.

The No-Good, Rotten, Run-On Sentence

BY LIZA CHARLESWORTH
ILLUSTRATED BY DOUG JONES

Do you know what a run-on sentence is? Share your ideas.

One day, Kevin Crabtree had a great idea for a story. But when he sat down to write it, the very first sentence refused to behave. It ran and ran and ran. In fact, it ran right off the page and out of his bedroom!

Grammar Tales

A

but sometimes they argued over which baseball team was best

But Kevin had to get his thoughts down, so he just kept writing. A minute later, he heard a crash. Then, his sister Darcy burst in. "What's the deal with that sentence?" she asked. "It ran through the kitchen and knocked over my cereal. Then it ran out the open window!"

B

---

11. ○ **U.** Kevin doesn't run after his sentences anymore. He runs on the track team instead!

○ **V.** Kevin doesn't run after his sentences anymore, he runs on the track team instead!

Now crack the code! Each number below stands for one of the questions. Write the letter of the correct answer above each number. Then read your secret message!

You don't let run-ons give you ___ ___ ___
                                10 4 3

___ ___ ___ ___ ___ ___ ___ ___ ___ !
 9 11 7 1 9 8 11 7 2

---

4. ○ **G.** Kevin chased after the sentence, his sister followed close behind.

○ **H.** Kevin chased after the sentence, and his sister followed close behind.

5. ○ **I.** Mrs. Smoodle's dog tried to catch it the run-on sentence was too fast for him.

○ **J.** Mrs. Smoodle's dog tried to catch it, but the run-on sentence was too fast for him.

6. ○ **K.** Cowboy Cal couldn't catch it, his lasso was too short.

○ **L.** Cowboy Cal couldn't catch it because his lasso was too short.

7. ○ **M.** Kevin ran as fast as he could, finally, he caught that pesky sentence.

○ **N.** Kevin ran as fast as he could. Finally, he caught that pesky sentence.

Rule Out Run-ons! Look at each set of sentences. Fill in the circle next to the sentence that is **not** a run-on. Then use the letters of your answers to decode the secret message at the end.

1. ○ **A.** Kevin Crabtree was bored, so he decided to write a story.
   ○ **B.** Kevin Crabtree was bored, he decided to write a story.

2. ○ **C.** He had a lot of great ideas, before he knew it he had written the longest sentence in the world!
   ○ **D.** He had a lot of great ideas. Before he knew it, he had written the longest sentence in the world!

3. ○ **E.** Kevin tried to keep his sentence on the paper, but it ran right out the front door.
   ○ **F.** Kevin tried to keep his sentence on the paper, it ran right out the front door.

and which was the most delicious kind of candy bar

> A sentence is a group of words that expresses a complete thought or idea. A run-on sentence crowds too many ideas into one sentence, or doesn't link them with proper punctuation.

Kevin put down his pencil. "I don't know what's wrong. My story idea is fantastic, but the first sentence just keeps going and going and going and going…"

"I think I get the idea. Don't worry. I'll catch it," replied Darcy, who was the fastest runner in all of Blathertown.

Kevin Crabtree
reads from
his bestseller,
***Melvin
the Monster***

Autographs
Saturday
10 AM–1 PM

"A modern masterpiece."
—J.D. Pine

> What have you learned about run-on sentences? Talk about it.

And that's exactly what she did. After that, Kevin never had a problem with a run-on sentence again. And his excellent story was published to rave reviews, with a great big dedication to dear Miss Bartlebine.

the monster's name was Bernard and he had orange polka dots on his back

> **Is this a run-on sentence?**
>
> The queen ate her pudding with a golden spoon from a golden bowl and was so very happy to have a pet pig named Gertrude, who loved pudding almost as much as pickles but not as much as apple pie.
>
> (Answer: yes)

Along came Mrs. Smoodle and her dog, Lightning. "What's all the commotion?" she asked.

"Kevin is writing a story and his first sentence will not stop," yelped Darcy. "I tried to catch it, but it just keeps running!"

still they had a great life until one day another monster knocked on the door

Darcy put on her running shoes and darted out the door. She passed a skateboarder and a biker and a bus. She huffed and puffed, but she just couldn't catch that no-good, rotten, run-on sentence!

C

Let's Review: Sentence Structure

Using proper sentence structure helps make ideas clear and keeps readers from getting confused. A run-on sentence happens when there is a mistake in sentence structure.

★ A sentence is a group of words that expresses a complete thought or idea. A run-on sentence is a sentence that tries to include too many ideas at once, making it "run on" way too long. Run-on sentences also occur when two or more sentences are linked together improperly, or without the correct punctuation.

★ One way to fix a run-on sentence is to divide it into two smaller ones. For instance: *The monster's name was Bernard, he had orange polka dots on his back.* That sentence can be divided into two separate ideas: *The monster's name was Bernard. He had orange polka dots on his back.*

★ Another possible way to fix a run-on sentence is by adding a word like *but, yet, for, because,* or *and.* For instance: *The monster's name was Bernard, and he had orange polka dots on his back.*

★ Remember, a run-on sentence doesn't have to be long! Any sentence that improperly links ideas, even short ones, is a run-on. Here's an example: *Come inside, it's raining.* Can you think of two different ways to correct it?

Bernard said that he was from France and needed a place to stay

"Oh my! That's soooo rude!" declared Mrs. Smoodle. "This sounds like a job for Lightning. After all, he's the fastest dog in all of Blathertown. He'll get that no-good, rotten, run-on sentence or his name's not Lightning-Sweetie-Pie-Shmoopie Smoodle III ." Then she pointed her finger at the sentence and commanded, "Fetch, boy!"

D

of orange spots on his skin. When he was done, he stood in front himself. Now, it was time to find Timothy. When Timothy saw Melvin, did those orange spots come from?" he exclaimed. Timothy was Melvin the Monster, especially his beautiful, red spotless skin.

Now it's your turn. Break this run-on sentence into a bunch of shorter sentences.

• The ice-cream truck played a happy tune it pulled up to Claudia's corner the good news was that she had 75 cents for a cone the bad news was that the ice-cream man was completely out of fudge-ripple-peppermint-strawberry swirl which happened to be her favorite flavor.

She then returned the pencil to her purse, declaring, "My work here is done. Now, let's go over and visit Kevin. I'd like to give him a little grammar lesson."

Melvin the Monster took a paintbrush and carefully dabbed hundreds
of the full-length mirror. "Wow, I really look different!" he said to
he was so surprised that he nearly hit the ceiling. "Where
very, very, very upset. You see, he loved everything about

"How did you do that?" Darcy exclaimed.

"Well, when a sentence keeps going and going, it becomes what is known as a run-on sentence. Run-on sentences are good sentences gone bad. Ideas get confused. Readers get lost. It's NOT a pretty sight," sighed Miss Bartlebine.

but there was really not enough room under the bed because
BROTHER
PIZZA
JONES

Is this a run-on sentence?

The king ate his pudding, it was quite tasty.

(Answer: yes)

As expected, Lightning took off like a flash. He passed a jogger and a roller skater and a pizza delivery truck, but it was no use. He just couldn't catch that no-good, rotten, run-on sentence.

After a while, Timothy started paying more attention to Bernard than Melvin. That
Then Melvin got a great idea. "I'll paint big, bright orange spots on my back too!"

"A pencil?" they exclaimed. "That's no match for the no-good, rotten, run-on sentence." Next, Miss Bartlebine did an amazing thing: She pointed the pencil at the sentence and started editing. She broke it apart into smaller sentences. She added capital letters and commas and periods and question marks and even an exclamation point or two.

Melvin thought of each one as a close personal friend

Which of these is a run-on sentence?

1. The clown with the rainbow wig and purple gloves, who had just joined the circus and was excited about it, juggled jellybeans and donuts.

2. The lion tamer did not go in the cage, it was way too scary in there.

(Answer: both)

"Why, I'll get that ornery, disrespectful gaggle of words if it's the last thing I do," said Cowboy Cal. He twirled his lasso this way and that and took expert aim. But to his surprise, that no-good, rotten, run-on sentence slipped right through the rope and kept on going!

there were so many dust bunnies under there and

Along came Cowboy Cal on his horse. "Howdy, partners. Why the long faces?"

"Kevin is writing a story and his first sentence keeps running and not even Lightning can catch it!" explained Mrs. Smoodle.

E

made Melvin get pretty jealous, but what could he do? he thought. That way, I'll be just as handsome as Bernard.

> Sometimes you can fix run-on sentences by adding a word like *but, yet, for, because,* or *and.* Can you fix these sentences with one of them?
>
> **1.** The woodchuck was always late to school, his alarm clock was broken.
>
> **2.** The chipmunk was funny, the squirrel was funnier.

Then before you knew it, that no-good, rotten, run-on sentence was no more. And in its place were dozens of tidy, clear, perfectly polite sentences—along with the start of a darn good story.

reluctantly Melvin decided to let Bernard stay as long as he agreed

"Look! It's heading for the center of town!" gulped Darcy. With no time to spare, the four of them hopped on Cowboy Cal's horse and galloped toward Town Square.

F

to hide under Timothy's bed when his mom came in

By the time they arrived, everyone had scattered to the safety of their homes. Everyone, but Dear Miss Bartlebine. "Watch out!" they screamed. "It's Kevin's no-good, rotten, run-on sentence!"

"Oh that silly thing," she replied calmly. "I'll take care of it." Then she reached inside her purse and pulled out a red pencil.

Proofreading

Background

Proofreading is an important step for any writer. Writers must check their work for mistakes in order to keep their meaning clear. Remind students to proofread for mistakes in capitalization (first words in sentences, proper nouns), punctuation (apostrophes, commas, periods, question marks, exclamation points), and spelling. It's important to emphasize that students should always proofread their work, whether they are writing a book report or an e-mail. Although some forms of writing are more informal than others, proofreading is the best way to make sure the message is clear. *Francine Fribble, Proofreading Policewoman* shows students the importance of proofreading as she reviews a variety of common errors.

Before Reading

- Introduce the importance of proofreading by showing students what your writing would look like without it. Write a class message on the board—such as a lesson plan—including mistakes in capitalization, punctuation, and spelling. For instance: *Todays lesson is on proofreading? check your work for misteaks in capitalization, punctuation, And spellig.* What is the first thing students notice about the message? Probably that it is riddled with errors! Would the lesson plan be difficult to follow? Explain that proofreading —double-checking your work and correcting mistakes—is important because it helps keep meaning clear. Errors can be distracting. If capitalization, punctuation, and spelling are correct, the reader can concentrate on the *meaning* of the words rather than the errors.

- Work with students to correct the message, pointing out the rules for capitalization, apostrophes, end punctuation, and spelling. Discuss important proofreading strategies, such as running a finger under each sentence to check for errors, looking up word spellings in the dictionary, and so on. Invite students to share any proofreading strategies they might already use.

•Next, show students the cover of the book and invite them to make predictions about the story. How will Francine help the people of her town?

During Reading

After reading the story once through for meaning, you can reinforce a variety of concepts in subsequent readings.

•Invite students to raise their hands each time they see an error in the illustrations.

•Help students distinguish different types of errors by inviting them to raise their hands only for spelling errors. Then try the same for punctuation and capitalization. Invite students to suggest corrections for each error they see.

After Reading

In addition to the group overhead lesson and mini-book practice activities, try the following extensions to help reinforce students' learning.

•Have a proofreading relay. Write a sentence on the board, including errors in capitalization, punctuation, and spelling. Have students form a line in front of the sentence. Give the first student a piece of chalk and invite him or her to make one change to the sentence (such as adding an apostrophe). That student then gives the chalk to the next person in line, who makes one more change (such as changing a lowercase letter to a capital). After students finish a turn, they go to the back of the line. Continue until students think the sentence has been completely corrected.

•Students can always proofread their work by crossing out (or erasing) errors and writing in their corrections. However, they might enjoy learning to use some of the proofreading marks that professional editors use to correct copy. Teach students a few basic marks and invite them to create a poster showing what each symbol means. For instance:

•A triple underline turns a lowercase letter into a capital: <u>c</u>hina

•A caret shows where to insert a word or a punctuation mark: Betty's

•A delete mark crosses out any letter, word, or punctuation mark to be deleted and ends in a curlicue: spe<del>e</del>lling

To Extend Learning

Use the activity on the next page to reinforce and extend the concepts students have learned. You can turn this into a collaborative whole-class activity by using the page on an overhead projector, or make multiple copies for students to work on individually.

•Have students read the directions at the top of the sheet. Then have them read the paragraph and point out the errors. Students can cross out mistakes and write corrections above the cross-out, as well as adding in any missing punctuation.

•Have students rewrite the story on the lines with their corrections in place.

Proofreading Police Work

When you proofread, check for mistakes in capitalization, punctuation, and spelling. Remember:

- The first word in a sentence should always be capitalized, as well as any proper nouns.
- Use an apostrophe to show possession. Check to make sure that each sentence ends with the correct punctuation mark.
- If you're not sure how to spell a word, look it up in the dictionary.

This story is full of mistakes! Check each sentence for errors. Then rewrite the story on the lines with the proper corrections in place.

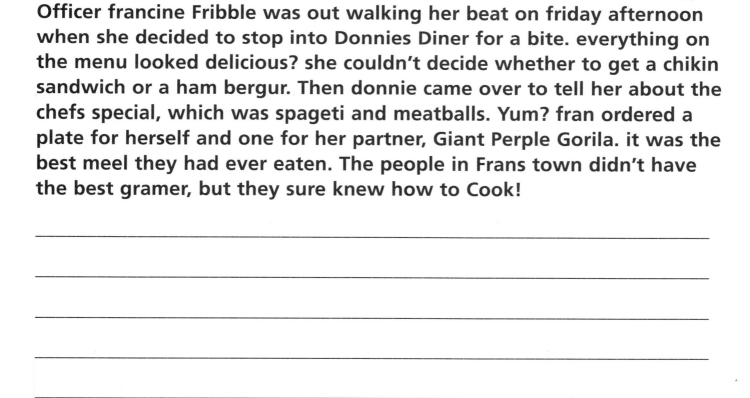

Officer francine Fribble was out walking her beat on friday afternoon when she decided to stop into Donnies Diner for a bite. everything on the menu looked delicious? she couldn't decide whether to get a chikin sandwich or a ham bergur. Then donnie came over to tell her about the chefs special, which was spageti and meatballs. Yum? fran ordered a plate for herself and one for her partner, Giant Perple Gorila. it was the best meel they had ever eaten. The people in Frans town didn't have the best gramer, but they sure knew how to Cook!

_____

_____

_____

_____

_____

_____

Try This!

A**||** writers make mistakes — the trick is to catch them and correct them. What kinds of mistakes do you make most often in your writing? Look over a few of your most recent stories or assignments. Proofread for mistakes in capitalization, punctuation, and spelling. Then make a personal checklist for yourself based on the errors you find. The next time you sit down to write, pull out your checklist. When it's time to proofread, you'll know what to watch out for!

Francine Fribble, Proofreading Policewoman

BY JUSTIN McCORY MARTIN
ILLUSTRATED BY JARED LEE

6. ○ **P.** Donnie thanked her and gave her a free chocolate doenut?

   ○ **Q.** Donnie thanked her and gave her a free choklit donut!

   ○ **R.** Donnie thanked her and gave her a free chocolate donut.

7. ○ **S.** If you ever pass through letterton, be sure to use good Grammar.

   ○ **T.** If you ever pass through Letterton, be sure to use good grammar.

   ○ **U.** if you ever pass through Letterton, be sure to use good gramer.

8. ○ **V.** If you don't proofread your T-shirt, officer fribble might give you a fine.

   ○ **W.** If you don't proofread your T-shirt, Officer Fribble might give you a fine.

   ○ **X.** If you don't proofread your T-shirt, Ofisir Fribble might give you a fine.

My name is Officer Francine Fribble. I'm with the Letterton Proofreading Police. My job is to help enforce the laws of grammar. When I see sloppy sentences, I fix them up with the proper capitalization, punctuation, and spelling.

A

---

9. ○ **Y.** But if you do get a ticket, you can be sure francine will spell your name correctly!

○ **Z.** But if you do get a tikit, you can be sure Francine will spell your name corektly!

○ **A.** But if you do get a ticket, you can be sure Francine will spell your name correctly!

Now crack the code! Each number below stands for one of the questions. Write the letter of the correct answer above each number. Then read your secret message!

When it comes to proofreading, you're on the

"___ ___ ___ ___ ___" ___ ___ ___ ___ ___!
  8   6   3   7   2   7   6   9   1   4

Folks around here have some pretty interesting things to say. Now, if they'd just take a little more time to check their work, communication would be a whole lot clearer. Then again, I'd be out of a job. Let's go make the rounds.

B

○ **H.** When the owner of donnie's Diner saw her coming, he tried to hide the menu.

○ **I.** When the owner of Donnie's Diner saw her coming, he tried to hide the menu.

4. ○ **J.** donnie made delicious food, but his grammar was awful!

○ **K.** Donnie made delicious food, but his grammar was awful!

○ **L.** Donnie made delishus food, but his grammar was awful?

5. ○ **M.** Officer Fribble gave him a warning and told him to proofread more carefully next time.

○ **N.** Officer fribble gave him a warning and told him to proofread more carefully next time,

○ **O.** officer Fribble gave him a warnig and told him to proofread more carefully next time?

Be a Grammar Cop! **Proofread each set of sentences. Fill in the circle next to the sentence that has no errors. Then use the letters of your answers to decode the secret message at the end.**

1. ○ **A.** Francine Fribble was the tuffest cop on the Letterton Proofreading Police force.

   ○ **B.** francine Fribble was the toughest cop on the letterton Proofreading Police force.

   ○ **C.** Francine Fribble was the toughest cop on the Letterton Proofreading Police force.

2. ○ **D.** She could spot a spelling misteak from a mile away.

   ○ **E.** She could spot a spelling mistake from a mile away.

   ○ **F.** she could spot a spelling mistake from a mile away?

3. ○ **G.** When the owner of Donnies diner saw her coming, he tried to hide the menu.

> **Proofread the club's sign. Can you find five things wrong with its capitalization? Turn the page for the answers.**

Well, what have we here? I'm on the beat for one minute and already I see a sign riddled with capitalization errors.

Well, time to sign off. This is Proofreading Policewoman Francine Fribble, and her new partner, Giant Purple Gorilla, reminding you to always check your work and correct the errors. That way, your writing will stay on the straight and narrow. And readers will know exactly what you mean to say.

> **Proofread the T-shirts. Can you find one thing wrong with the punctuation on each? Turn the page for the answers.**

Yikes, look at that lineup! When T-shirts are in trouble, Officer Francine Fribble is on the case.

> **The first letter of the first word of any sentence always gets capitalized. The names of people, like *Bill*, and organizations, like the *Iguana Club*, get capitalized, too.**

Here you go, kids. Now you are members of the Good Grammar Club, too!

C

Let's Review: Proofreading

Proofreading is an important step for any writer. Checking your work for mistakes in capitalization, punctuation, and spelling helps keep your writing clear.

★ Check to make sure that the first word of each sentence begins with a capital letter. Make sure that you've also capitalized the first letter of any proper nouns, such as names of people or organizations (*Billy*, *Iguana Club*).

★ You should also look for mistakes in punctuation. Remember to include an apostrophe to show possession (*Betty's Burger Palace*). Make sure that the ends of your sentences have the correct punctuation, too. Periods, question marks, and exclamation points help readers understand the meaning of a sentence. A football fan who shouts, *Go Spartans?* sounds very different from one who shouts, *Go Spartans!*

★ Spelling mistakes can also confuse meaning. A reader may not know what a *ham berger* is, but will certainly recognize a *hamburger*! If you're not sure how to spell a word, look it up in the dictionary.

★ When should you proofread? Always! Whether you're writing a book report or an e-mail, double-checking your work is the best way to make sure your message is clear.

> **Complete sentences should always end with the perfect punctuation mark. Also, words that show possession, such as *Betty's* or *world's*, need apostrophes to make their meaning clear.**

Now, that's what I call clean laundry. With my help, the T-shirts are crisp, comfy, and error-free.

D

I think I'll give this Super Toss a try. Wow! I won! I won! I won! By the way, what did I win?

> What strategies do you use to help you proofread your work? Share them with others.

Talk about being a corrections officer! A proofreading policewoman's job is never done.

> Proofread the menu. Can you correct the spelling of each word? Turn the page for the answers.

All this proofreading is making my stomach growl. Time to stop for a bite at Donnie's Diner. Uh-oh! Take a gander at all the misspellings on this menu. Why, there ought to be a law! I guess my little doughnut break will just have to wait.

> Whether you're writing an e-mail or a message in the sky, proofreading your work is a must to get your point across.

Fortunately, I'm a licensed skywriter. Now, everyone will get the message. Hmmm…a fair sounds like a blast, and tomorrow just happens to be my day off.

> Proofread the note. It has a total of nine errors in capitalization, punctuation, and spelling. Can you find them all? Turn the page for the answers.

Now, what have we here? Someone's left a note on my scooter. It sure is hard to understand. But one thing's for certain. Someone needs my help, pronto!

> When words are misspelled, their meanings can get lost. If you're not sure how a word is spelled, you can turn to a friend or the good old dictionary.

I'm always happy to aid a citizen in need. Yum! By the way, this double-chocolate-dipped, jelly-filled, strawberry-cinnamon-swirl doughnut with rainbow sprinkles really hits the spot!

E

> Proofread this sign. It has a whopping ten errors in all! Can you pinpoint them all?

The game looks like honest entertainment, but that sign is just plain criminal.

> All writers make mistakes. To help find yours, try running your finger under each word as you proofread it.

Now that Toodles is safe and sound, let's take a peek at your note. It needed some help, too. I took the liberty of making a few corrections.

F

> Proofread the skywriting. Can you find nine things wrong with this airborne advertisement?

I'm a ten-year veteran on this force. Still, every day I see something new. Take a look at that skywriting! Why, it's loaded with errors! Just because those words are floating ten thousand feet in the air, doesn't mean the rules don't apply to them.

Answer Key

Nouns: Chicken in the City
Name that Noun! (Overhead, page 15)

Name That Noun!

Nouns can name people, animals, places, things, ideas, and feelings.

Find the nouns in each sentence.
- Circle the nouns that name people or animals.
- Draw a box around the nouns that name places.
- Draw one line under the nouns that name things.
- Draw two lines under the nouns that name ideas and feelings.

❶ (Lu-Lu) the (chicken) was bored with life on the [farm].

❷ She longed for the excitement of the big [city], so she packed her suitcase and got on a bus.

❸ Her (friends) were sorry to see her go, but they wished her luck as they waved good-bye.

❹ (Lu-Lu) had a lot of fun on her adventure—she bought a pretzel from a vendor who was selling all sorts of food on the [street].

❺ She couldn't find the [museum], so she asked a (police officer) for help and he gave her a map.

❻ (Lu-Lu) decided that she missed the green grass and blue skies of the [country], so she went back [home].

❼ But she was glad she had brought her camera—the (cows) laughed with delight when they saw the pictures she took at the [zoo]!

A Box Full of Nouns
(Mini-Book, page 18)

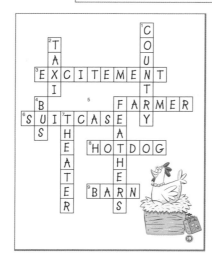

Be a Noun Detective (Mini-Book, page 20)
farm; place; chicken; hay; cows; friend; hands; trip; Hen; Hotel; view; city; nest; food; menu; eggs

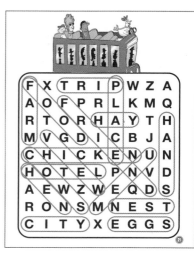

Verbs: A Verb for Herb
Where's the Action? (Overhead, page 25)

Where's the Action?

Verbs

A verb can describe either an action or a condition. Verbs that describe actions are called *action verbs*. Verbs that describe conditions are called *linking verbs*.

Find the verb (or verbs) in each sentence.
- Underline the verbs that describe an action.
- Circle the verbs that describe a condition, or state of being.

❶ Herb (was) very bored.

❷ He <u>sat</u> in a chair all day long, (feeling) blue.

❸ At last, a fairy <u>flew</u> through the window.

❹ "You (are) quite a sorry sight," she <u>said</u>.

❺ But she <u>knew</u> just what Herb <u>needed</u>.

❻ She <u>pulled</u> a verb out of her sack, and Herb (was) ready for action!

❼ He <u>painted</u> beautiful pictures and <u>wrote</u> amazing stories.

❽ After a lot of <u>running</u> and <u>jumping</u>, Herb (was) all tired out.

❾ So he <u>crawled</u> into bed with a book—his new favorite (is) the dictionary!

Take another look at the sentences above. Make a tick mark in the chart for each action verb and each linking verb you find. How many of each type did you find all together?

Action Verb	Linking Verb
11	6

Help Wanted!
(Mini-Book, page 18)

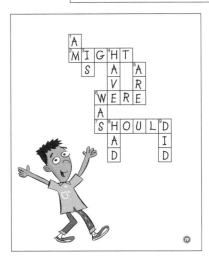

We're Going on a Verb Hunt (Mini-Book, page 20)
are; go; will; lead; can; find; drive; see; might; swim; is; leave; be; take

Adjectives: The Bug Book
Adjectives All Around (Overhead, page 35)

Adjectives All Around

Adjectives

An adjective is a word that modifies, or describes, a noun or a pronoun.

Read the sentences below.
Underline each adjective you see.

❶ Ten enthusiastic bugs decided to throw a wild party.

❷ They decorated their tiny house with long, colorful streamers.

❸ They invited many friends—big bugs, small bugs, short bugs, and tall bugs.

❹ They wanted to be friendly hosts, so they even made the grouchy bugs feel welcome.

Read the sentences below. Circle the noun that each underlined adjective modifies.

❺ When they brought out the giant cake all the bugs were happily surprised.

❻ The ladybugs were especially pleased, because it was covered with red icing and black chocolate chip dots!

❼ Zany insects love wacky parties!

Read the sentences below. Sound boring? Add adjectives to each sentence to make it more detailed and interesting. Write your new sentence on the line.

❽ The bugs played music.

_____Answers will vary._____

❾ The centipede wore shoes.

_____Answers will vary._____

❿ The beetle spilled a drink on the rug.

_____Answers will vary._____

Rhyme Time
(Mini-Book, page 18)

Go Buggy!
(Mini-Book, page 20)
special; good; buggy; fabulous; favorite; complete; party; festive; many; floral; delicious; hungry; lovable; spectacular

Adverb Adventures

Adverbs

An adverb is a word that modifies, or tells more about, a verb, an adjective, or another adverb. An adverb can tell you how, when, where, or to what extent.

Find the adverbs in the sentences below.
- Underline the adverbs that tell you how.
- Circle the adverbs that tell you when.
- Draw a box around the adverbs that tell you where.
- Draw two lines under the adverbs that tell you to what extent.

❶ Tillie plays her tuba <u>very</u> <u>loudly</u>.

❷ (Yesterday,) she took her tuba [outside] and performed <u>enthusiastically</u> for the birds.

❸ But the birds found the noise <u>really</u> annoying, so they asked her to <u>kindly</u> cut it out.

❹ Tillie was <u>extremely</u> insulted and <u>tearfully</u> put her tuba [away.]

Read the sentences below. Circle the word that the underlined adverb modifies.

❺ "I'll play a concert for my goldfish!" Tillie (thought) <u>excitedly</u>.

❻ But the goldfish thought the concert was <u>completely</u> (awful.)

❼ "The violin might be <u>far</u> (less) annoying," he suggested.

Read the sentences below. Rewrite each sentence so it contains at least one adverb. Write your new sentence on the line.

❽ Tillie played her tuba with pride.

Possible answer: Tillie played her tuba proudly.

❾ She practiced on it without end.

Possible answer: She practiced on it endlessly.

❿ But she was happy to switch to the violin.

Possible answer: But she happily switched to the violin.

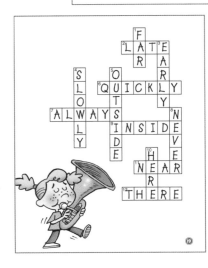

How's That?
(Mini-Book, page 20)
constantly; away;
simply; terribly;
endlessly; nowhere;
today; patiently; soon;
proudly; sweetly; now;
absolutely; never

Pronouns: The Planet Without Pronouns
Super Stand-Ins
(Overhead, page 55)

Super Stand-Ins  Pronouns

A pronoun is a word that "stands in" for a noun. Many pronouns name people or things. Some pronouns also show ownership.

Find the pronouns in each sentence.
- Circle the pronouns that name one person or thing.
- Draw a box around the pronouns that name more than one person or thing.
- Underline the pronouns that show ownership.

❶ Stanley built (his) own spaceship and rode (it) to a distant planet.

❷ (He) decided to explore Krimular and see what (it) was like.

❸ (He) met some friendly aliens, but (he) found [them] very strange.

❹ [Their] sentences were so long and complicated that (he) could barely understand [them].

❺ "(I) know what's wrong!" (he) cried. "[You] don't use pronouns!"

❻ "(I) will teach (you) how to make sentences shorter," (he) told Zik.

❼ "(My) friends and (I) would love to learn," Zik replied.

Read each sentence below. Circle the noun that the underlined pronoun is standing in for.

❽ As he began his lesson, Stanley told the (aliens) that <u>they</u> needed to pay attention.

❾ So the aliens gathered around the (blackboard,) but they were so excited that they almost knocked <u>it</u> over.

❿ When the lesson was over, (Stanley) told the aliens that <u>he</u> had to go back home.

Placing Pronouns
(Mini-Book, page 18)

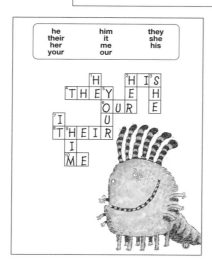

Pronouns on Parade (Mini-Book, page 20)
your; you; We; our; It; me; They; I; them; their

A Capital Caper

Capitalization

Names of specific people, places, and things begin with a capital letter. The beginning of a sentence is always capitalized. So is the pronoun *I*.

> The story below has 21 capitalization errors. Can you find them all?
> • Underline the uncapitalized words that SHOULD be capitalized.
> • Circle the capitalized words that should NOT be capitalized.

Cindy was running out of ideas for her science fair project. So far, she had tried out three different inventions, and each one was a disaster! Her brother zeke thought she should invent a new kind of cereal. But when she tried out a box of garlic goodies on her family, nobody seemed to like them much. cindy's Father suggested she invent a robot to clean her room. But the robot kept misplacing things—Cindy still couldn't find her autographed copy of alien Adventures, and it was her favorite book! mrs. Cadoodle wanted Cindy to invent an automatic baseball pitcher. she thought it might help her favorite Team win the championship. But the manager of the springfield tigers said that only human players were allowed. "How will i ever come up with a new invention by next friday?" Cindy thought. Just then, she got a postcard in the mail from her friend lucy Lowercase, who had moved to louisiana in september. There were no capital letters in Lucy's note! The Postcard gave Cindy a wonderful idea. She got straight to work on her new machine—she knew she would amaze Mr. menlo and all the students at sunny street School!

Comma Conundrums

Commas are used to separate items or ideas in a sentence.

> **Read each sentence below.**
> • Write in any missing commas. • Cross out any unnecessary commas.

❶ Before Comma came to town, people's sentences were very long.

❷ One boy told his friends that his favorite ice cream flavors were peach, chocolate, vanilla, strawberry fudge-ripple, and butterscotch.

❸ The town bakery sold cakes, cookies, pies, and bread.

❹ Comma thought that the land of And was the nicest, friendliest, prettiest place he'd ever seen.

❺ He knew he could help the townspeople, although it would take a lot of work.

❻ The townspeople wanted to thank Comma, so they threw him a party.

❼ Comma wished he could stay in the town forever but he had many other places to visit.

❽ Ned the town fish sadly waved his fin goodbye.

❾ Comma wished all the townspeople good luck, good health, and good grammar!

Join the Comma Club! (Mini-Book, page 18)
   1. B; **2.** E; **3.** I; **4.** K; **5.** N; **6.** R; **7.** S; **8.** W; **9.** A

Message: Now you're using "comma sense"!

Quotation Marks: The Mystery of the Missing Socks
Quotation Locations (Overhead, page 85)

Quotation Locations

Quotation Marks

Quotation marks show the exact words that someone says.
Remember these rules:

- Quotation marks are placed before and after the speaker's words.
- Quotations begin with a capital letter unless they continue a sentence.
- A comma separates the quotation from the words that tell who is speaking.
- Periods are placed inside the ending quotation marks.
- If the speaker's words end with a question mark or an exclamation point, it is placed inside the ending quotation marks.

Read each sentence below. Insert quotation marks in the correct places.

❶ "I need a report on Mr. McGillicutty's missing socks for tomorrow's paper," Steve's boss said.

❷ "Don't worry," said Steve. "I'm an expert on missing socks. I'll get right on it!"

❸ "Can you tell me exactly what your socks looked like?" Steve asked Mr. McGillicutty.

❹ Mr. McGillicutty answered, "They were extra large and had polka dots."

Read each sentence below. Insert any missing quotation marks. Insert any missing commas.

❺ "If anyone likes polka-dot socks," said Mrs. Slice, "it's Harold."

❻ "That's true," Jenny Jennings said. "But Harold likes any kind of socks!"

❼ "Harold once tried to take my socks right off my feet," said Mike Montey.

❽ "Arf, arf," said Harold.

Quotation Marks Mark the Spot (Mini-Book, page 18)
1. A; 2. D; 3. E; 4. H; 5. I; 6. K; 7. M; 8. P; 9. R; 10. T

Message: You really hit the mark!

Sentence Structure: The No-Good, Rotten, Run-on Sentence
Run-ons Run Wild! (Overhead, page 95)
Possible answer:

Kevin Crabtree decided to write a new story. This one was about a monster named Gertrude the Gabber. No one listened to Gertrude at the Monster Meetings because she talked too much. Everyone said that her sentences went on and on. There was just no stopping her! Then she met a monster named Edwin the Editor. He told her all she needed was a pencil to shorten her sentences. Gertrude didn't believe him, but she tried it at the next meeting. Now Gertrude is an excellent speaker, and she's also the Monster Club's new secretary!

Rule Out Run-ons! (Mini-Book, page 18)
1. A; 2. D; 3. E; 4. H; 5. J; 6. L; 7. N; 8. O; 9. R; 10. T; 11. U
Message:
You don't let run-ons give you the runaround!

Proofreading: Francine Fribble, Proofreading Policewoman
Proofreading Police Work (Overhead, page 105)
Possible answer (end punctuation may vary):

Officer Francine Fribble was out walking her beat on Friday afternoon when she decided to stop into Donnie's Diner for a bite. Everything on the menu looked delicious! She couldn't decide whether to get a chicken sandwich or a hamburger. Then Donnie came over to tell her about the chef's special, which was spaghetti and meatballs. Yum! Fran ordered a plate for herself and one for her partner, Giant Purple Gorilla. It was the best meal they had ever eaten. The people in Fran's town didn't have the best grammar, but they sure knew how to cook!

Be a Grammar Cop! (Mini-Book, page 18)
1. C; 2. E; 3. I; 4. K; 5. M; 6. R; 7. T; 8. W; 9. A
Message:
When it comes to proofreading, you're on the "write" track!